NO MORE SHACKS!

"All of God's people
should have at least a simple,
decent place to live."
—Millard Fuller

NO MORE SHACKS!

Millard Fuller
with
Diane Scott

The daring vision of Habitat for Humanity

WORD BOOKS
PUBLISHER
WACO, TEXAS

A DIVISION OF
WORD, INCORPORATED

NO MORE SHACKS!

Scripture quotations in this publication are from
Today's English Version of the Bible (TEV), copyright
© American Bible Society 1966, 1971, 1976.
Used by permission.

Scripture quotations marked NASB are from the New American Standard
Bible, © The Lockman Foundation 1960, 1962, 1963, 1968, 1971, 1972,
1975, 1977.

All author proceeds and royalties from the sale of this book
are being used to help eliminate poverty housing
through Habitat for Humanity.

Library of Congress Cataloging in Publication Data:
Fuller, Millard, 1935–
    No more shacks!

    1. Habitat for Humanity, Inc.   2. Housing.
3. Poor.   I. Scott, Diane, 1933–   .   II. Title.
HV97.H32F85   1986   363.5'763   86–13209
ISBN 0–8499–0604–0
ISBN 0–8499–3050–2 (pbk.)

            67898   FG   987654321

Printed in the United States of America

This book is dedicated to Robert L. Wood of Westport, Connecticut. One of my dearest friends and a founding director of Habitat for Humanity in 1976, Bob tirelessly gave of himself to the emerging vision of this ministry. While Linda and I were writing the first draft of this manuscript, Bob went home to be with the Lord he loved and served so faithfully.

—MILLARD FULLER

CONTENTS

Foreword

Shalom is a word that the ancient Jews used in their greetings and in their farewells. To the Hebrew people of biblical times, it meant much more than our interpretation of "peace." Shalom meant total spiritual and physical well being. It called up visions of a society perfectly ordered by Yahweh, marked by love and justice. Shalom was life as God had meant for it to be. It was a world in which the needs of every person were met and where each one had enough of whatever was required to live a joyful life before the Lord.

Jesus initiated His ministry by declaring that the kingdom of God was at hand (Matt. 4:17). By the kingdom of God, He meant a world in which all that was suggested by shalom would be realized. This kingdom was to be composed of people delivered from sin and guilt, and freed to love one another. It was to have its social institutions reshaped according to the will of the heavenly Father, and would be a society marked by justice, offering to all peoples everywhere the opportunity to live with dignity. Its citizens were to be spiritually "reborn" through the transforming work of One who was not *of* this world, and they were to be *in* this world as agents through whom God would change the world from what it is into what it ought to be. Millard Fuller is a citizen of the kingdom. And he is one of the instruments through which the kingdom of God is manifesting itself among us.

By the time he was thirty, Millard had fulfilled the aspirations of every yuppy. He was a millionnaire with all the things millionnaires should have: a huge house, a beautiful wife, cars, clothes, and everything else that goes with "the good life." Millard was always a man who had respect for the church and faith in God, but it was not until he took literally the command of Christ to give up all of his wealth for the sake of the poor that he became a disciple. Here is a man who has come to understand what Deitrich

9

Bonhoeffer meant when he said, "When Jesus calls a man, He bids him come and die." And so Millard and Linda sold what they had, gave it to the poor, and followed their Lord.

For the Fullers, and for those who would join them in carrying out their vision, the way in which they live out the requisites of the kingdom of God is to help poor people to have decent housing. They started a movement called Habitat for Humanity, and today that movement is providing expressions of shalom for people around the world. Thousands of people in towns in Africa, cities in America, rural settings in Asia, and suburbs in Latino societies have found help and hope from this movement. This book is only a small part of the story of the continuation of that movement, but it is bound to inspire readers to action for others in the name of the Lord.

Like a mustard seed, Habitat for Humanity started small. And, like a mustard seed, it has the potential to grow large enough for all the birds of the air to nest in it. Habitat for Humanity is a part of the good news for the poor declared by Jesus. It is one expression of God's kingdom, one manifestation of shalom. Let those who have eyes to see, see! God is doing a great thing through the Fullers and through their movement. *No More Shacks!* is an opportunity to get a glimpse of their vision and an invitation to participate.

TONY CAMPOLO

ACKNOWLEDGMENTS

My wife, Linda, and I started gathering material for *No More Shacks!* soon after *Love in the Mortar Joints* was published in 1980; the actual writing began in June 1985. I worked almost continuously through the summer and into October. Then Diane Scott of Salem, New Jersey, took over. She demolished what I had written, eliminating some sections, rewriting and rearranging others, and adding two new chapters. In February and March of 1986 Diane and I together completed the final manuscript. What you will read is very much the product of our combined efforts, along with excellent suggestions from Linda, who typed and retyped the ever-changing chapters, and from Diane's husband, Vic.

Words are inadequate to thank Diane and Linda for their tremendous contributions. Diane, who earlier worked with me on *Bokotola* and *Love in the Mortar Joints*, deserves enormous credit for her role.

Many other people contributed in various ways to the creation of *No More Shacks!* Among them are:

John and Chrys Street, who offered their cabin near beautiful Lake Rabun, Georgia, so that Linda and I could begin writing this book in June of 1985.

Jimmy and Rosalynn Carter and John and Betty Pope, who also graciously made their cabin in North Georgia available to Linda and me while we were working on the manuscript.

Susan Ausley, and her daughters Margaret Hoffman and Elisabeth Gablehouse, who later provided a cabin at St. Teresa Beach near Tallahassee, Florida, for still another quiet writing place.

Rachel Hoblin, Carolyn McGarity, and Barbara Garvin, my able volunteer assistants in Americus, who provided diligent research and proofreading.

Wallace Braud, Habitat's Media Director, who helped Linda keep her word processor going, and the Media Center staff, which supplied maps and pictures.

The entire Habitat office staff in Americus, who assisted in too many ways to list, but I am particularly grateful for their steadfast encouragement and prayers. We sensed and appreciated these every day over the months of writing.

Unnumbered Habitat folks around the world, who cheerfully gathered information and photographs for us, and answered streams of questions about their projects.

And the good people at WORD, Incorporated, who provided the finest spirit of cooperation which could possibly exist between an author and a publisher.

Habitat for Humanity has always been a partnership. It is a partnership between each one of us in this ministry and God; it is also a partnership between us and the families receiving the houses. *No More Shacks!* is one result of this great partnership, and all of us who worked on it have been blessed.

Now I hope that it will bless and inspire you as well.

1

No More
Shacks!

April 6, 1985, was a pleasantly mild spring Saturday in Americus, Georgia. It was also the day before Easter. At ten o'clock in the morning, four hundred people gathered on Habitat Street to dedicate three recently completed houses. Former president Jimmy Carter had worked with the Habitat for Humanity crew on one of the houses, and he and Rosalynn were there to share in the celebration.

Among the crowd assembled around the speakers' stand we had set up on the sidewalk were reporters, new homeowners, construction volunteers, office staff, friends from nearby Koinonia Farm, local supporters, and other Habitat folks from all over. As I scanned the faces of so many friends, I recognized representatives from a dozen cities in Georgia as well as at least five other states.

There was an air of happy expectancy. Our excitement was heightened by graphic reminders of why we were there. Just a stone's throw away on Church Street, in full view of everyone, was a row of typical South Georgia shacks—no paint, no insulation, holes in the walls, roofs caving in, front porches falling off. Two of the families whose new houses we were dedicating today had just moved out of those shacks. The third family had come from a tiny rented basement under the back side of an old house built on a steep bank; it was located in another section of Americus.

To express the joy we all felt, Frances Parks, a local Habitat partner, stepped to the microphone. She had written a song called "Love in Action" especially for the occasion, and her clear, strong soprano voice rang out unaccompanied.

> Rejoice, brothers and sisters!
> We've something to celebrate!
> We have Habitat for Humanity,
> And we don't have to wait . . .
>
> Until we enter the next world
> To enjoy the benefits
> Of the promises of Jesus,
> And the beauty of His gifts.
>
> 'Cause we have love in action,
> Love in action!
> It consoles the heart,
> Fulfills the soul,
> And brings satisfaction.
> Habitat is love in action.
> It fulfills the need,
> And without greed
> Brings about interaction.

Frances kept returning to her refrain: "Habitat is love in action." People began nodding and smiling; soon they were humming and clapping. At the conclusion of her song, applause and cheers reverberated up and down the block.

A few moments later, Jimmy Carter came to the microphone. Chuckles rippled through the crowd as he started his talk by acknowledging how difficult it was to follow Frances Parks! Then he began to speak more seriously. Simply and earnestly, Jimmy Carter described the significance for him of involvement in Habitat for Humanity.

"I've had many experiences in my life and in Christian work, in business, government and politics. I've traveled almost everywhere in the world, and I don't know of anything I've ever seen that more vividly illustrates love in action than Habitat for Humanity. It's inspirational and practical; it draws people together who've known each other for a long time in a special way; it makes new friends for you every day that you work with Habitat; and it's a challenge because you never know what's going to happen next.

"I've had a lot of people ask me, 'Why did you and Rosalynn get involved with Habitat, with all the other things that come to you as opportunities—exciting things, world-wide things? Why did you choose Habitat?' Well, that's not an easy question to answer in a hurry, but there are a few things that I feel to be particularly important.

"The federal government, the state and local governments, have just about all they can handle. Sometimes they don't do enough; sometimes the taxpayers think they do too much. Habitat encourages the federal government to have good housing programs. And private enterprise can build houses and sell them for profit. But Habitat is kind of the 'frosting on the cake.' It's the additional contribution that is having a rapidly growing impact on poor people without homes. So I like that part of it.

"Another thing I like about Habitat is that it's not a handout. We don't embarrass people by saying, 'I'm a rich person, and I'm going to give you poor folks something for yourselves.' Instead, it's a partnership. It's not somebody up here helping somebody down there. It's somebody reaching out a hand and saying, 'Let's work together.' And the family that is helped has a new experience, a great challenge—getting rid of an old house and putting up a new one. That's one of the greatest achievements in the lives of many poor families who have never seen a decent home from the inside. . . . There's a new sense of pride, dignity, determination. In the process, not only do they learn how to pour concrete, lay bricks, build roof trusses and walls, and fix up the grounds around the house, but they also feel that they've accomplished something on their own. And they see what partnership can do. They've seen what, in Christian love, working together can do. I like that part of it as well.

"And the last thing I like about Habitat is the international scope of it. The goal of Habitat is that every time we build a house in the United States, we build at least one house overseas. We are now building more than one home per day for people in need. That is a very exciting thing. Rosalynn and I have been to only one Habitat project overseas, in Puno, Peru, right on the edge of Lake Titicaca at an altitude of thirteen thousand feet. And it was inspirational to go there and see how those people are making a new life for themselves. But that's going on now in twelve other countries, and the applications for Habitat to come into even more countries are just stacking up, and all of us can help. Well, you can see how much I love Habitat. . . .

"I was in New York this week. I got up early to jog, which I like to do before the sun comes up. There's not much traffic, and people don't come up and bother me—much—but there are still people sleeping on the streets, on the concrete sidewalk. A lot of them only have a towel or a coat or a newspaper between their human face and a filthy sidewalk. And some of them are older women, without any place in the world to sleep at night except on the streets. That's in the richest city in the richest nation on earth.

"The need is everywhere. And I think Jesus Christ, our Savior, wants us to do something about it. That's what Habitat is doing. In the name of Jesus, love in action. That's why I'm proud to be part of it. Thank you."

Warm and prolonged applause followed President Carter's words. His obvious sincerity and commitment encouraged us all.

Then I ascended the little sidewalk stage to share what was on my heart. I had wrestled for days with what I would say. But only a short time before the dedication service, as I walked from my home half a mile away, I had settled on the message I wanted to deliver.

"This morning I have three important words for you. The three words are these: *No more shacks!* That's what Habitat is about: No more shacks! Say it with me: *No more shacks!*"

I began to yell the three words over and over in rhythmic beats. The crowd picked up the chant, and clapping and shouting in unison they cried, "No more shacks! *No more shacks! NO MORE SHACKS!*"

The cheer was repeated several more times. Then it gradually died down, and I began trying to express the mixed emotions of celebration and challenge which welled up within me.

"You know, I have never met a person who lived in a house that leaked and they liked it. I have never met a person who lived in a house that didn't have insulation, and when the cold days came they couldn't get warm, and they liked it. I have never met a family who lived in a house with great holes in the floor that you could throw a cat through or great holes in the ceiling that you could see the stars through and they liked it. Never! But we have people here in Sumter County living that way. Habitat for Humanity is all about changing that.

"We believe that with God all things are possible. We believe, therefore, that poverty housing can be eliminated in Sumter County, Georgia. No more shacks! We must all begin to say that it is unacceptable—religiously and socially and politically—for people to be living in subhuman conditions. When we see people living in houses that leak and that don't have insulation, we need to say within ourselves, 'We care so much, we're going to do something about it.' We don't have shacks because there's not enough money. We have shacks because there are not enough people who care enough to make it an unacceptable situation!

"Habitat is saying in dedication services here in Americus, and up in Atlanta, and in Syracuse, and Tucson, and East St. Louis, and Evansville, and Tallahassee, and in all these other places, 'We believe that with God we can change things. We can make things better. We can reach across the boundary line of our own personal lot where our house is situated; we can reach across the boundary line which separates us from the next city; we can reach across the boundary line that separates our state from the next state. Indeed, we can reach across the boundary which separates our country from other countries, and say that we care so much that we're going to reach out and do what we can with the resources that God has given. Because it is unacceptable for some people to be living in great affluence while others are living in abject poverty.' We have got to change things, and with God we can change things, and glory halleluia, praise the Lord, we *are* changing things! That's what it's all about.

"No more shacks! They're unacceptable! No more shacks! But how are we going to get rid of the shacks? There's a lot more to it than just getting excited at a rally. This is fun. I love standing up here and yelling, 'No more shacks!' But if you just yell, there are no houses getting built. When the yelling is over, you gotta pick up the hammer and start driving the nails.

"This afternoon we're going to drive nails right down the street from here. There's a house being built by the Americus Habitat Committee for Mae Pearl Denmark. Mae Pearl is here, and she doesn't mind my telling you this. She didn't have anywhere to live. The family that lived in the corner shack, Willie and Dorothy Solomon, now live in this new house. It's one of the three we are dedicating today. So Mae Pearl Denmark moved into their old shack, because it is so much better than where she was living. But praise the Lord, a good house is under construction for Mae Pearl Denmark and her children. It's right around the curve here, and if you come this afternoon, you won't be building a house *for* Mae Pearl Denmark; she'll be right there with you. She will help you drive the nails, saw the boards, and carry the lumber. That's what Habitat's all about—building *with* people, working *with* them. It's partnership. It's partnership with God Almighty in heaven and it's partnership with our brothers and sisters on earth."

And that's how we are going to get rid of the shacks.

2

An Idea Explodes

The thought came to me in an interview on a Sunday morning talk show on radio station KGO in San Francisco. I was in the midst of a ten-day speaking trip, which included several appearances in each of eight western cities. It was April of 1981

I had been traveling rapidly from one state to the next, marveling at the endlessly varied shades of springtime around me. God was unfolding a different display at every stop I made, offering the world His annual explosion of April colors. But on that particular Sunday morning, it was an idea that exploded.

The radio show, which aired from six to nine, had begun typically enough with an interview about the growing ministry of Habitat for Humanity, then five years old. At that time we were building and renovating homes for needy families at eleven locations in the United States and five more in third world countries. And new groups were forming all the time.

Tom Hunter, a United Church of Christ pastor, hosted the

weekly program, and we discussed Habitat for about ten minutes. He then invited listeners to call in their questions. One person inquired about the types of homes we construct; another was interested in the method of repayment and the default rate; a third asked how, since we accept no government funds, we could obtain enough money to build so many houses. I spent some time explaining to this last questioner that we operate on faith and depend on God's people to provide both funds and volunteer labor.

When I answered the next call, a woman's voice asked simply, "What is the goal of Habitat for Humanity?"

No one had ever asked me that precise question. But from the depth of my soul, I immediately knew the answer.

Without hesitation, I replied, "To eliminate poverty housing from the face of the earth."

That's it, I realized. *The whole vision.* For years we'd been saying we were going to eliminate poverty housing in Sumter County, Georgia, where Koinonia Partners had been building homes for poor families since 1969. It was at Koinonia, in fact, that the idea of Habitat for Humanity was born.

And in more recent years, as people began to hear about Habitat projects launched by groups in other parts of the United States and around the world, more and more folks were starting to say, "We can do it here, too!" The whole concept was catching the imaginations of ever-enlarging numbers of people; lives and lifestyles were being radically altered, as dramatically among those who pitched in to help as among the families who were being helped.

But now the big picture had suddenly snapped into sharp focus. Our goal, I realized at that moment, is not to build a handful or even hundreds or thousands of homes in Georgia or New Hampshire, or Guatemala, or Zaire. *Our goal is simply to eliminate poverty housing from every state in the United States and from every country in the world.*

The woman gasped on the other end of the telephone line. Then there was silence.

I continued. "And when we get rid of all the poverty housing,"

I informed her confidently, "we'll start on something else!"

She gasped again. Then she gave a faint laugh, and without another word she hung up.

Immediately the station's phones started ringing off the hook.

"What a fantastic idea! How can I get involved?"

"Where did you say you're from? Please give that address again."

"My neighborhood needs this desperately—do you have a mailing that will give me more information?"

The boldness of this goal, I discovered, had really stirred people. They wanted to be a part of such a movement. They had caught a vision: By putting hearts and hands together in this practical expression of love for God's people in need, they could actually make a difference. They could help eliminate poverty housing throughout the world.

A few days later I returned to the Habitat office in Americus, exhilarated and energized by that morning on the talk show—which was a good thing. If we were ever going to reach the goal I had just announced over the radio, there was a lot of work still to be done!

In the weeks and months that followed, I began to preach about this goal in speaking engagements all over the country. "It's time to get rid of the shacks! Everywhere!"

And while I was absolutely certain that this was the direction God was leading us with Habitat's ministry, I was doing a lot of serious thinking. I had to have solid answers for the inevitable question: "How in the world are you going to reach that enormous goal?"

For me, the answers were clear. But I was constantly searching for new opportunities to share them with others. This book is one result of that search.

The simplest answer I can offer to the question of how to eliminate poverty housing in the world is to make it a matter of conscience. We must do whatever is necessary to cause people to think and act to bring adequate shelter to everyone. And we'll do this through a spirit of *partnership*.

First, we're in partnership with God. If Habitat were primarily a movement of individuals, there would be nothing lasting to it. But this is God's movement, and there's nothing that can stop it.

Second, we're in partnership with each other. One of the most exciting features of Habitat for Humanity is that people who don't normally work together at all are coming together everywhere to work in this cause: the affluent and the poor; high school students and senior citizens; conservatives and liberals; Roman Catholics and Protestants; and every racial and ethnic group you can think of. We might disagree on how to preach or how to dress or how to baptize or how to take communion or even what communion is for. But we can all pick up a hammer and, sharing the love of Christ, we can begin to drive nails. Thank God we can agree on a nail!

With this dual partnership as our foundation, we are going to arouse the consciences of individuals and organizations around the world, challenging them to join in this cause. And together, we are going to get rid of the shacks. *All of them!*

David Rowe, president of the International Board of Directors of Habitat for Humanity, is pastor of the First Baptist Church of Melrose, Massachusetts. During the fall of 1985 David and his wife, Bonnie, led a weekend work group from their church to the Habitat project in Portland, Maine. Working in partnership over those two days to raise a roof for the first Habitat house in Portland were twenty-three people. The youngest was ten, the eldest was eighty.

Habitat folks in Portland had begun to place their witness to the love of Christ right where it was needed: on a vacant, littered corner in the midst of a decaying neighborhood. They were well along on their first house, a duplex, when five carloads of short-term volunteers drove from Massachusetts to Maine on a chilly Saturday morning in September.

As they pulled up in front of the building site, the visitors were greeted by some large letters, the work of an anonymous local person wielding a can of spray paint. Some graffiti is quotable; David thought this one was positively inspired. So do I. Stretched across the side wall of Portland's partially constructed house were the scornful words HABITAT FOR INSANITY.

If insanity means doing things in ways that are unexpected, unusual, even unacceptable to large segments of society, then Habitat cheerfully accepts that description. Volunteers are giving months and years of their lives. Supporters are giving enormous chunks of their cash. High-salaried professional people are giving their time and their skills. Poor families are giving their own "sweat equity." A former president of the United States and his wife are donning work overalls and giving weeks of manual labor. And everyone involved is giving thanks. Homes are being built all over the world. No profit is being made by anyone, and homeowners are charged no interest. No question about it—to most people, this whole operation sounds crazy.

In the first century A.D., a small group of people who kept following an itinerant rabbi long after his death were mockingly called "Christians." When this hardy band began spreading all over the earth to carry out their commission, they were still faced with derision, and often much worse. All the while they steadfastly pursued their foolish goal of changing the world. In the twentieth century, Habitat for Humanity, another group of determined Christians, is working faithfully toward another outrageous goal: eliminating poverty housing from the face of the earth.

At our fall 1985 board meeting in New York City, David Rowe related the graffiti episode in Portland, and he urged us never to "abandon our insanity." Instead, he said, we have to "stay crazy, be nuts, act abnormal, look out of place, think 'off the wall,' try the unacceptable—as the world sees it—until we change the perspective of the world!"

Back in September of 1976, a group of twenty-seven friends and supporters of the concept of partnership housing came together at Koinonia Farm near Americus. They represented eleven states and many Christian groups. After three days of deep discussion and prayer, Habitat for Humanity was brainstormed into existence. During one of our devotional times at that meeting, I challenged the participants with a quote from Daniel Hudson Burnham, an outstanding American architect at the beginning of this century:

> Make no little plans, they have no
> magic to stir men's blood. . . .
> Make big plans . . . remembering that a
> noble logical diagram, once recorded, will
> never die, but long after we are gone
> will be a living thing, asserting itself
> with ever-growing insistency.[1]

Habitat for Humanity is making big plans.

---

1. *Burnham of Chicago, Architect and Planner* by Thomas S. Hines (second edition, Chicago: University of Chicago Press, 1974), 401.

3

Koinonia: Habitat's Birthplace

The idea of building houses for the poor using biblical economics—seeking no profit and charging no interest*—originated at Koinonia Farm. Koinonia (the Greek word for *fellowship*) is a Christian community southwest of Americus. The distance between what is now Habitat Street in this small Georgia town and Koinonia Farm is only eight miles. But the band of people and experiences which connects these two places keeps getting longer and longer. It now stretches around the world.

I first went to Koinonia in 1965, at a time of deep personal crisis. My wife Linda and I had become almost totally estranged. She had left me in November of that year and had gone to New York City to think about our future together, or if we would even have one.

We had been living in Montgomery, Alabama, where I was immersed in a successful direct mail and publishing business that

* Exodus 22:25

25

had been started as a partnership with another student at the University of Alabama Law School in Tuscaloosa. For eight years, he and I had been developing the company, and it had grown to the point where we were each making a hundred thousand dollars a year in salary. My personal net worth was over a million dollars. I lived in a lovely home, drove a Lincoln Continental, and had a cabin and speed boats on a nearby lake. With my partner, I owned two thousand acres of pasture land for our riding horses and herds of cattle.

Linda and I had just about everything material that a young couple could possibly desire. But we learned that possessions alone do not bring happiness, nor do they give meaning to life.

After a time of agonizing separation, I followed Linda to New York. A period of soul-searching, confession, and prayer ensued and a long reconciliation process began. We realized our lives had gone astray, and we felt a strong desire to come back to the Lord and to find His plan for us. To prepare ourselves for this new start, we were led to sell our business interests in Montgomery and give all the money away.[1]

Linda and I arrived at Koinonia Farm that December planning to visit for a couple of hours. We ended up staying for a month. Our personal healing process, which was just beginning, was aided tremendously by Clarence Jordan, who had been one of the founders of Koinonia with his wife, Florence, back in 1942.

I was captivated by this man. Never before had I encountered such commitment to Christ. Under Clarence's leadership, Koinonia had begun as a "gathered" fellowship patterned after the early Church, with a specific mission of teaching improved agricultural methods to impoverished local tenant farmers. Practicing non-violence, sharing possessions, and welcoming all races, the residents were not accepted by their white neighbors. Over the years they had been beaten, shot at, burned out, boycotted, and mistreated in every conceivable way. Yet they had never retaliated. They had unfailingly struggled to return love for hate.[2]

The Bible gives clear instructions about this, said Clarence. (And he knew the Scriptures well. Combining his degree in agriculture from the University of Georgia and his Ph.D. in Greek New Testament from Southern Baptist Seminary, Clarence had almost completed his best-selling *Cotton Patch* versions of the New Testament[3] when he died suddenly in 1969.) Despite the world's dependence upon armed force, with each nation eager to be strong enough to crush all the others, Clarence insisted that we must return to Jesus' way: Love your enemies; do good to those who persecute you; turn the other cheek; go the second mile.

"That doesn't make sense from the secular perspective," Clarence admitted, "but we're God's people. He gives us the strength to love our enemies—and even to help them if we get a chance."

Clarence's steadfast faithfulness to the gospel was incomprehensible to most of Koinonia's neighbors. He often reminisced about an incident that took place during World War II, just as the farm was getting established. A local farmer stopped by and angrily accused the handful of residents there of being unpatriotic.

"That's not true at all," replied Clarence. "You've been given some wrong information."

"But you people won't fight!"

"On the contrary," Clarence said. "We're *big* fighters."

"You are?" The farmer looked puzzled.

"Yes," Clarence went on, and he started to tell him about the armor and weapons of God, but quickly realized that talking theology to the fellow would go right over his head. So he tried another tack.

"Don't you have a mule over at your farm?" Clarence asked.

"Yeah. You know I got several."

"Well then," Clarence went on, "let me ask you a question." Clarence had a mule at Koinonia named Hyacinth, and most farmers throughout the south at that time depended on these sturdy animals for field work.

"What would you do if you were walking by your barn, and your mule suddenly stuck his head over the gate and bit you on the fanny?"

"I'd pick up the nearest two-by-four and clobber him."

"Now, why would you do that?"

"'Cause I wouldn't let no mule get away with bitin' me!"

"But why wouldn't you bite him back? That's what he did to you."

"*Bite him!* You crazy? I ain't gonna bite no mule. What on earth are you talkin' about?"

Clarence always smiled at the recollection of the man's incredulity.

"Fighting. And what to fight with! That's what I'm talking about. You don't let the mule choose the weapon for you. You choose your own weapon. Christians can't let the forces of evil choose the weapons we fight with, either. The world chooses bombs and guns; we choose love and kindness and forgiveness."

Whenever he saw the world and the Word at odds with each other, Clarence refused to compromise.

"In Christ there is neither Jew nor Greek, slave nor free, male nor female—we're all one in Him.* And in South Georgia," Clarence reminded us, "that means that in Christ there is neither black nor white. The world is teaching us to stay apart—but the Word of God says come together. And we'll follow God's Word!"

On one occasion, Clarence's dogged faithfulness to Jesus led an unhappy preacher to seek some advice. His congregation, he said, had made it impossible for him really to preach the gospel. They simply wouldn't stand for it. The clergyman sadly told Clarence that he had begun to feel like a paid performer who had to say and do whatever his church members wished.

Clarence looked at the man intently.

"What you are saying, Brother, is that you feel like a whore!"

The preacher swallowed hard.

"Yes, I suppose I do."

"Then why don't you quit?"

"Well, uh—I really don't know anything except pastoring. All my training is in theology. What would I do?"

Clarence continued to look his questioner squarely in the eye.

"I don't know, Brother," he replied. "If a whore knows nothing but whoring, does that justify her remaining in the profession?"

On the subject of biblical economics, Clarence's message was equally unmistakable.

"The world says, 'Lay up riches for yourself, so you can be financially secure, enjoy the good life, and eventually retire on a comfortable pension.' Jesus says, 'Don't store up riches for yourselves here on earth, where moths and rust and robbers can get at them. Store

---

* Galatians 3:28

up your riches in heaven, where they're safe!'*

"That simply means," said Clarence, "that if we're following Jesus, we share whatever we have, and we trust Him for the rest."

I was profoundly affected by the teaching of this man of God. A scholar and a humorist, Clarence was brilliant and yet thoroughly down-to-earth. His compelling preaching was in demand all over the country, but Clarence was most at home at Koinonia Farm in his faded overalls, sharing stories about the "God Movement," Clarence's term for the kingdom of God. During our family's month-long stay at Koinonia, Clarence and I talked together for hours on end. He realized that my spiritual well had run dry, and he was willing to be used by God to refill it.

In 1968, after Linda and I had worked for two and a half years in other full-time Christian endeavors, we decided to move to Koinonia Farm. The decades of persecution and struggle had taken their toll on the community. Although seekers of all ages still visited Koinonia to work for various periods, by the time we arrived that summer only two other families were living there year round.

Despite sporadic violence and a boycott by local merchants, Koinonia had managed to hold on to one asset—eleven hundred acres of land. Throughout our area, however, poor tenant farmers were frequently being forced to leave their hardscrabble rural life for a still more precarious existence in the cities. And in either place, people ended up huddled together in dangerously decrepit dwellings. They had no hope of ever acquiring a decent place to live.

In August of 1968, Clarence and I called together at Koinonia a group of fifteen spiritually sensitive and socially aware Christians. Out of this four-day conference came a new vision, to be called Koinonia Partners. And a major segment of this ministry would be Partnership Housing. In a letter to the large mailing list of supporters around the country whose gifts and no-interest loans had enabled Koinonia to survive the years of persecution, Clarence described a radically new kind of housing program.

We have laid off forty-two half-acre home sites and are making them available to displaced rural families. Four acres in the center are

* Matthew 6:19–21

being reserved as a community park and recreational area. We will put up a four-bedroom house with bath, kitchen, and living room, and this will be sold to a family over a twenty year period with no interest, only a small monthly administration charge. Thus the cost will be about half the usual financing, and for a poor person this can be the difference between owning a house and not owning one. The interest forces him to pay for two houses, but he gets only one.

The partner family will gradually free the initial capital to build houses for others, and will be encouraged to share at least a part of their savings on interest with the fund that built their house. Even as all are benefited, so should all share. If, as Jesus says, "it is more blessed to give than to get," then even the poorest should not be denied the extra blessedness of giving.

The money for this building program would be raised, Clarence explained, through the inauguration of a Fund for Humanity.

What the poor need is not charity but capital, not caseworkers but co-workers. And what the rich need is a wise, honorable, and just way of divesting themselves of their overabundance. The Fund for Humanity will meet both of these needs.

Money for the fund will come from shared gifts by those who feel that they have more than they need, from no-interest loans from those who cannot afford to make the gift but who do want to provide working capital for the disinherited, and from the voluntarily shared profits from the partnership industries, farms, and houses. As a starter, it has been agreed to transfer all of Koinonia Farm's assets of about $250,000 to the Fund. Other gifts are already beginning to come in.

The Fund will give away no money. It is not a handout. It will provide capital for the partnership enterprises.

Clarence died just a year after this great effort was undertaken. He was fifty-seven. He was sitting in his "shack," a little one-room study there on the farm, laboring over one of his powerful sermons one afternoon when his Lord called him home.

The shock of his death, at first overwhelming to all of us who loved him, served to strengthen our commitment to the unfolding vision of Partnership Housing. God had called us, through Clarence, to meet a mighty challenge.

With the assistance of several more families who had been drawn to the community by the new undertaking, and with the gifts and no-interest loans of hundreds of friends elsewhere, the first housing site of twenty-seven homes was virtually complete and occupied by late 1972. Some lots had been reserved for recreation areas, and two more were used for a child development center and a nursery. We had already laid out another tract for thirty-two houses about a mile down the road.

The following year, another challenge beckoned. Under the auspices of the Christian Church (Disciples of Christ), and in association with the United Church of Christ, Linda and I left Koinonia to accept a special missionary assignment in the heart of Africa. With our four children we traveled to France for language study, and then on to Zaire. We were determined to test the partnership housing concept in a third world country. A 1966 trip to Mbandaka, the capital of equator region in Zaire, had convinced us this city was a good place to start. The area teemed with miserable squatter settlements thrown up after the people won their independence from Belgium in 1960, when they were suddenly free to move from their jungle villages to the city. In little more than ten years, Mbandaka's population had ballooned from thirty thousand to one hundred and fifty thousand. Decent housing for any but the very well-to-do was rare, and for the newcomers it was nonexistent.

For three years Linda and I wrestled with problems and discouragements ranging from thievery, a ludicrous bureaucracy, capricious arrests, and a perpetual shortage of funds and materials, to cultural adjustments like learning to be patient in a land where time means very little. But we were blessed with a succession of extraordinary volunteers to work with us, as well as the support of hundreds of Christian friends back home. And once the local citizens in their falling-down shacks discovered we were serious about helping them to construct solid houses which they could actually own, their enthusiasm knew no bounds.

Pastor Lokoni's crumbling mud house at the edge of Mbandaka sheltered (sort of) nine children whom he and his wife had taken in to raise as their own. He was a fantastic encourager of the project. And something he once told visitors at our work site expressed his wonder and excitement.

"Years ago," he said, "when the missionaries came, the first thing they did was build nice houses for themselves. Next, they built nice houses for God. But they didn't help the people build houses!" He went on to explain that he believed God had sent Linda and me, and the volunteers, to build houses for the people. "Ask anybody. They'll tell you that housing is our biggest need. It's *magnifique* that the church is building a new community right here in the center of the city!"

When we left Zaire on July 4, 1976, eighty families were making their monthly payments into the Mbandaka Fund for Humanity, and hundreds of people had already moved into their new houses. Plans were underway for a second project in the village of Ntondo, ninety miles to the south. There, just three families were living in homes made of durable materials; the local committee had agreed that everyone else in the village needed decent housing, and therefore we would have to build *three hundred houses*. That would clearly be a vast undertaking. We had no idea where the money would come from. But the Lord had gone with us every step of the way, and we knew He wouldn't let us down now.[4]

When Linda and I returned to Koinonia Farm in 1976, the question filling our minds was: *Where does God want us to go from here?* With the birth of Habitat for Humanity that fall, our direction became clear. This new organization would raise funds, recruit volunteers, and provide procedures and expertise to develop around the world a better habitat for God's people in need.

The dream had been launched. We had no idea how fast it would take off.

---

1. Our experiences during this time are recounted in *Love in the Mortar Joints* (Piscataway, NJ: New Century Publishers, 1980).
2. See *The Cotton Patch Evidence* by Dallas Lee (New York: Harper and Row, 1972).
3. *The Cotton Patch Version of Paul's Epistle* (© 1968), *Luke and Acts* (© 1969), and *Matthew and John* (© 1970) were published by Association Press; *Hebrews and the General Epistles* (© 1973) was published by Koinonia Partners.
4. The complete story of our stay in Zaire is told in *Bokotola* (New York: Association Press, 1977).

A typical shack in Americus, Georgia.

Workers tear down a shack to make room for sturdy new houses.

Volunteer David Scherger lays block for a new Habitat house in Americus, Georgia. (Photo by Bill Moore.)

Above: Former president Jimmy Carter inspires listeners at the dedication of a new house.

Below: Habitat housing is gradually replacing the broken-down shacks in this poverty-stricken neighborhood.

Left: Breaking ground for the first Habitat house in Garrett County, Maryland. Right: Carrying supplies to a building site in Gulu, Uganda.

Left: Hard at work building Habitat housing in Peru.

Dedication of new homes in Tucson, Arizona *(left)* and Puno, Peru *(right)*.

Right: Millard sits with Al Zook *(left)* and Clarence Jordan *(right)* at Koinonia—1969.

Left: First house completed at Koinonia Village— 1969.

Millard works with nationals on the construction of the first house in Mbandaka, Zaire *(right)* as youngest daughter Georgia looks on *(left)*— 1974.

4

The Size of
the Problem

When we organized Habitat for Humanity at Koinonia Farm in 1976, determined to enlarge our attack on the problem of poverty housing, we hadn't really considered how enormous that problem was. In the intervening years, the worldwide need has been documented in all its awesome proportions.

The United Nations Center for Human Settlements estimates that between one and one-and-a-half *billion* people, one quarter of the world's population, lack adequate shelter. Of these, approximately one hundred million have no housing whatever. In many cities in the third world, half of the people live in slum and squatter settlements. In some cities, over three-fourths of the population live in such conditions. In Latin America alone, it is estimated that twenty million children live in the streets, with no place to call home.

These poverty-stricken people often have limited access to water.

And most of them have no toilet facilities. The fortunate ones live in cramped rooms with walls made of cardboard, a piece of rusty metal, or mud poked between cornstalks and sticks; their roof may be a hodge-podge of tin, palm branches, tar paper, and tattered plastic. The unfortunate ones huddle in doorways or under bridges, or find no shelter at all.

In the developed nations, even though the problem of inadequate shelter is not nearly as severe as it is in places like Africa, Latin America, and much of Asia, there are still millions of people who suffer in living conditions which are not suitable for humans.

In New York City, where the Habitat for Humanity project on the Lower East Side of Manhattan has renovated a six-story building for nineteen low-income families, an estimated thirty to sixty thousand people are homeless, with two hundred and fifty thousand more on the brink of homelessness. The New York Housing Authority reports that nearly twenty thousand families have moved in with other families in public housing. Over one hundred and seventy thousand more families are on a waiting list to get in. The governor's office estimates that half a million people in the city live in substandard housing.

In Boston, where a new Habitat project was approved in April of 1985 to operate under the umbrella of the ecumenical agency Christians for Urban Justice (CUJ), more than five thousand people are homeless. Seven thousand families are waiting for public housing, and countless others have doubled or tripled up to avoid becoming homeless. Fourteen thousand abandoned housing units in Boston await renovation. The urban pastors who serve on CUJ's board of directors say flatly that *housing is the most pressing need in the inner city.* The target area for CUJ and the new Habitat project in Boston includes a census tract that is poorer than any other in the nation, except for the Mississippi Delta.

On the west coast, in Los Angeles, more than thirty thousand people are homeless. Thousands more are crowded into inadequate shelter. Substandard housing is a serious problem in every large city in the United States. However, similar needs in rural areas are often what drove people to the cities in the first place.

Throughout the Mississippi Delta, along the eastern banks of the river and stretching out into the fertile plains of northwestern Mississippi, thousands of people are trying to survive under conditions equal to those in Third World regions. Ray Hunt, founder of Habitat South, the Regional Center of Habitat for Humanity for that part of the country, estimates that fifteen thousand houses in the Delta are substandard, lacking plumbing, toilet facilities, insulation, or even structurally sound walls and roof. Several Habitat projects are already underway in this needy area in cooperation with the Christian relief and development agency World Vision, but the task before us is enormous.

In Sumter County, Georgia, where the idea of Habitat for Humanity was born, Habitat and the Partnership Housing program of Koinonia Partners have built over two hundred homes for low-income families. A dent has been made in the problem, but at least five hundred more dwellings are needed just in Sumter County (population 27,000) to put everyone in a decent house.

Appalachia Habitat for Humanity in Morgan and Scott Counties, Tennessee, has built, renovated, or repaired over one hundred houses, but there still remain countless families in that area who live in leaky shacks without even outdoor toilet facilities.

Throughout the United States, it is conservatively estimated that twenty million people live in substandard housing or have no housing at all. As a percentage of the population, that figure is small (less than 10 percent), but when we realize that this country is the richest in the world, we can only hang our heads in shame.

The size of this problem today is staggering. Big even in the United States, overseas it is colossal. And what about the future?

The United Nations estimates that the world's population will increase by one-and-a-half billion by the year 2000. Furthermore, it is predicted that 80 percent of these newcomers will be city dwellers, most of them in the developing countries. The population of slum and squatter settlements in these cities is increasing four times faster than world population growth. To understand the magnitude of the coming challenge, consider the effort necessary to build housing for one hundred twenty cities the size of New York in less than fifteen years!

On the African continent, the total population in 1970 was two hundred and seventy million. Ten years later it was three hundred and fifty-nine million. Predictions are that this figure will double by the year 2000 and triple by 2020, with at least eight African cities having over five million inhabitants each.

Worldwide, a billion people now live in cities. By the end of the century that figure will double, with half of the population in Third World countries living in cities. Five hundred million of these urban residents will be crammed into about sixty cities. Thus, unless heroic efforts are launched, the misery of city dwellers will be compounded in incredible ways. Scarce resources will be stretched even thinner. Life will become unbearable. Is there a solution to this ever-increasing problem?

At the beginning of 1986, Habitat for Humanity had modest projects underway in twenty-five locations in fourteen developing countries. Many of these projects were in cities—Kinshasa, Kikwit, Mbandaka, Basankusu, and Gemena, Zaire; Gulu, Uganda; Puno and Juliaca, Peru; Khammam, India; Port Moresby, Papua New Guinea. Hundreds of houses for poor families have been built at these sites, and more are going up every day. The value of these projects, however, is infinitely greater than the number of completed houses might indicate. Each new Habitat house becomes a beacon, a shining example of what Christian love in action can accomplish. These simple Habitat homes send a silent but significant message to everyone, rich or poor, who knows about them. Our intent is to enormously expand the number of these projects in the years ahead.

We are well aware, however, that Habitat for Humanity cannot solve this huge problem alone. Former president Jimmy Carter, an active board member of Habitat for Humanity, clearly explained Habitat's vision in an interview which appeared in the December 1984 issue of our quarterly newspaper, *Habitat World:*

> There is no way that Habitat can build all the homes that are necessary in the world. And what we'll have to do in the relatively near future is to decide not only how Habitat fits within the existing structure of home building, private investors, independent families with the capacity to build, state and federal programs here and in other countries, international organizations like the United Nations and the World Bank, and other benevolent groups, but we'll also,

in addition to that assessment, have to decide how Habitat's concept—which I think is unique, and effective, and inspiring—can be used to generate similar efforts throughout the world that won't be directly associated with Habitat at all. My own inclination is that Habitat should not concentrate its efforts in too large a degree in one particular community or even in one particular nation, but that we should implant the Habitat seed in the most needy places that we can identify, and let the Habitat program be, in effect, a pilot effort that could be emulated by others.

What I'm talking about is—do a limited number of Habitat projects in a particular region and then try to encourage private investors and government officials and others to emulate what we're doing.

This is what Habitat wants to do. Plant projects all over the world; sow seeds of hope, encouraging the poor to do all they can to help themselves; and cultivate consciences among the affluent, urging them, privately or corporately, to join less fortunate folks in a spirit of partnership, to solve the problem together.

Unfortunately, this effort is confronted with two major obstacles. One is an uncaring attitude on the part of people who could help. The other is the population explosion.

Even in the poorest Third World nations, there are numerous wealthy people. Few of them are known for their generosity toward their needy countrymen. Indeed, their attitude is most frequently characterized by a cold aloofness. Their plush living quarters are generally surrounded by high walls and armed guards; and the owners' interests lie mainly in protecting and increasing their personal possessions.

I recall once traveling on a plane from Kinshasa to Mbandaka, Zaire. I was seated next to a wealthy Zairian businessman. He knew who I was, and I knew of him. He started talking to me about the housing program in Mbandaka. After asking several questions about how the project operated, he announced, "Monsieur Fuller, I would like to have you build me a house."

I responded by reminding him that our project was for the poor, and that he certainly was not in that category.

"Well, of course you know," he volunteered, much to my astonishment, "I already have four houses. I would like you to build me another." He beamed.

"Citoyen," I addressed him, using the courtesy title employed in Zaire, "a lot of concerned people in the United States, Canada, and Europe have given money for building these houses for the poor. Since you are quite wealthy, I'd like to ask *you* to donate to the project, to help your own poor countrymen have better housing."

He was amazed. He fixed me with a long stare and then retorted, "I'm not interested in giving money away. I want to make more!"

In the Western world, we have a tradition of helping the poor. The basis for this is, of course, the Bible. A thousand years before the birth of Christ, God was reminding His people to be generous with their countrymen:

> If there is a poor man with you, one of your brothers, in any of your towns in your land which the LORD your God is giving you, you shall not harden your heart, nor close your hand from your poor brother; but you shall freely open your hand to him, and shall generously lend him sufficient for his need in whatever he lacks. You shall generously give to him, and your heart shall not be grieved when you give to him, because for this thing the LORD your God will bless you in all your work and in all your undertakings (Deut. 15:7–8, 10, NASB).

Unfortunately, an increasing number of affluent people in the West are opting to do what their wealthy counterparts are doing in developing countries. They build walls around themselves to keep the poor away. They don't share. Religious folks among the wealthy theologize that God has blessed them. They say they worked hard or that their parents or husband or wife worked hard, so they deserve all the possessions they have, and they are entitled to the luxurious lifestyle they enjoy. They feel no obligation to share significantly with others.

Recently an article in the *Atlanta Constitution* described a rich young man whose income was a million dollars a year. He had just built himself a plush mansion. The article also revealed that he was a Sunday school teacher. When he was asked about his great wealth in light of his Christian commitment, he replied that God had given him the talent to make money, and that justified his using it on himself. There was not a word about sharing anything.

While I was on a visit to a Habitat project in Nebraska, my host drove me past the new six-and-a-half-million-dollar home of a local business tycoon. It was enormous, surrounded by a high fence. I was told the owner had installed buzzers in the house so family members could find each other!

The king of the real estate companies selling fancy properties to the rich is headquartered in Denver, Colorado, with eleven other U.S. offices and associates on every continent in the world. Their annual guide, *Previews, Inc.*, is considered the "Blue Book" of real estate. It goes to executives of *Fortune* magazine's one thousand biggest companies and to officers of the world's three hundred and fifty largest banks. Quarterly supplements show new listings.

A bimonthly companion publication, *Homes International*, offers another dose of opulence. The prices of homes sold by this company are incredible. They say, for instance, that seldom does their Los Angeles office list anything below $700,000. The Denver office doesn't like to accept anything less than $400,000. Many of their properties sell for millions of dollars. One house recently sold for $19,000,000!

Previews, Inc. reports that increasingly people want to get away from urban problems. Furthermore, the company reports another trend is clearly apparent: *Instead of one large house, many people prefer now to have four or five homes.*

Another way Americans have found to avoid the problems of the poor is to go *up*. The December 9, 1985, issue of *New York Magazine* reported on a new super-luxury apartment building in the city called Metropolitan Tower. The public relations man for this sixty-five-story black glass edifice insists that it offers "the greatest views in the history of the world." It is certainly true that from that height, residents will have difficulty seeing dirt or poverty or homeless people sleeping on the sidewalk.

Metropolitan Tower shows prospective buyers a film of a woman in a pink towel sensuously enjoying a steam room massage, along with her toy poodle. The advertising is designed, said the article, "to persuade rich people to have fun with their money, to spend it blatantly. . . . The cheapest apartment in the house, a one-bedroom somewhat larger than a crevice, costs $320,000. The deluxe penthouse will go for a mere $5,000,000." In 1986, Habitat for Humanity was building simple homes in Bolivia, Nicaragua, and India for slightly more than $1 per square foot, and dozens of families were able to obtain decent shelter for the first time in their lives. That same year in New York City, the most expensive luxury apartments cost an average of *$700 per square foot.* These high-rise hiding places from the world's problems were selling briskly, while far below them thousands of homeless people wandered the city's streets.

Rich Americans too often build walls or put distances between themselves and the poor. Old John the Baptist, who cried in the wilderness twenty centuries ago to share that extra coat and food and other possessions with the poor,* has lost a lot of his congregation. Many people are too busy piling up coats and houses and other fancy belongings to turn their faces and hearts toward the folks who are piling up in the world's hovels. There is no question that the uncaring attitude on the part of the world's affluent is as much a part of the problem we face as is the plight of the poor themselves.

A national executive of a wealthy Protestant denomination, whose support I had requested for Habitat, once told me simply that, with all of the other needs in the world, "Housing is just not a priority with our mission board."

This attitude struck me as a strange double standard, because I had visited in the man's home shortly before this conversation. His house must have cost at least $150,000. In *his* life, housing had a very high priority!

Somehow, we must break into the consciousness of the rich in such a way that they change their perspective and become concerned about sharing the burdens of the poor. Standing alone, the poor can never solve their enormous shelter needs.

Furthermore, it must be understood that "rich" does not necessarily mean super-rich. Westerners in general are fantastically wealthy in comparison to most people in developing countries. It is not at all uncommon for a married couple in North America

* Luke 3:11

to earn together over $100,000 a year in salary. With these huge incomes, people are upgrading their living situation and spending enormous sums of money on housing for their families. For example, the median sales price for single-family homes in major metropolitan regions of the United States in 1985 was $73,900. In Los Angeles, the price was $114,300. In the New York City area, where thousands of people were in substandard housing, the *median* price of a house was an astronomical $125,400, and in Orange County, California, it was even higher—$132,100!

Even at these prices, more and more people in the United States are buying houses. In 1940, 60 percent of all families were renters; by 1985, a full 65 percent of all Americans owned their homes. Furthermore, for nearly a hundred years the number of houses has grown faster than the population, with the result that the average number of persons per household has declined. The number of people per house in the United States in 1985 was only 2.8.

The contrast between this situation and the housing scene in the third world is startling. Habitat for Humanity projects overseas are building two-, three- and four-bedroom houses of four hundred to a thousand square feet, for a cost of between $1,000 and $3,000. From five to fifteen or more people will move into each of these dwellings. This modest housing, with no plumbing, no electricity, and an outdoor toilet is a dramatic improvement over the shacks where the people were formerly forced to live.

Angelino Chipano is president of the Habitat project in Alto Beni, a low lying tropical area in the northern part of Bolivia. He described what life is like in their traditional houses made of bamboo walls, thatched roof and dirt floor.

> For seven months of the year it rains nearly every day. The rain comes right into the houses, between the bamboo that forms the walls. Everything gets soaked, and stays soaked until the dry season comes again. Sometimes the ants come. Three or four nights ago a whole colony of red ants invaded our house. The entire army got in my bed. I woke up in the middle of the night with ants all over me, all in the sheets, in my hair and clothes—everywhere.

In the affluent West we are inclined to spend vast sums of money on creature comforts. Over half of the nearly ninety million houses in the United States have air conditioning—and we live in the temperate zone. Our poorer brothers and sisters in the tropics can only hope for an open window to catch a slight breeze now and then.

Churches are as guilty of self-indulgence as are individuals. In my speaking tours around this country I am often grieved by plush houses of worship, and by the ungenerous spirit they exemplify. Once I presented Habitat at a church in Florida on the day they dedicated a new Sunday school wing. It cost $800,000.

Following the service, the pastor put his arm around my shoulders and effusively praised Habitat's ministry.

"God bless you," he intoned. "We are going to support this fine work. I'll be putting a check in the mail to you next week."

He did. Three days later we received $35. We never heard from that church again.

Certainly, many churches are not like this. Indeed, thousands of congregations generously support the work of Habitat for Humanity and other vital Christian endeavors. Unfortunately, however, there are thousands more who worship in lavish facilities allocating but a pittance to ministry for others. "I was a stranger . . . hungry . . . thirsty . . . naked . . . sick . . . in prison—and you voted to build another Sunday school wing, buy a bigger organ, and put in thicker carpet."

Take a look at your church budget. How much of it does your congregation spend on itself? Your church may be increasing the size of the problem!

In regard to population growth, there is no question that improved living conditions have the effect of limiting family size. The primary reason for having large families in the Third World is simply the need for retirement insurance—some of the children must survive in order to take care of their aging parents.

Studies in the United States have shown that improvements in living conditions here in the last century have been largely responsible for better health, and we are finding that the same is true in Habitat projects around the world. Once when I was in Ntondo,

Zaire, a British Baptist nurse exclaimed to me, "You are doing more for the health of these people with these houses than we've done with our clinic in the past twenty-five years. You are getting rid of the causes of many of their illnesses!"

As the mortality rate for children declines, and as people move into solid houses which belong to them, they will feel more secure about their situation. And they will not feel a desperate need for more and more offspring.

Another factor influencing population growth is widespread ignorance of how to limit family size. As concerned, educated people move in to work with the poor, helping them solve their basic need for shelter, fast friendships are formed. Then people become willing, even eager, to accept ideas on how to reduce the birth rate. Moving away from people and putting up higher walls is not the answer to this serious problem.

A final factor which must be considered when we examine the size of the problem is a historic failure to recognize the importance of shelter in the overall scheme of development for Third World countries. A 1984 World Bank publication, *Toward Sustained Development in Sub-Saharan Africa*, extensively discussed the importance of programs in education, health, population, agricultural research, and forestry. *The book did not even mention shelter needs.* It recognized the necessity to develop Africa's human resources, but failed to note any connection between this objective and improved housing.

All of the factors discussed in this chapter—the magnitude of the worldwide need, the population explosion, the self-centeredness of the affluent, and the failure of many to recognize the connection between adequate shelter and overall development—combine to present a challenge of massive dimensions. But with God, all things are possible. With His help, we can respond to this challenge.

I am constantly impressed by the involvement in Habitat of countless people who have realistically assessed the magnitude of this problem, and who are undaunted. Rather, they eagerly accept the challenge. And they have the vision to take bold steps.

Back in 1978, a dynamic pastor named Jack Takayanagi read

Bokotola. Jack, who grew up during the forties in the Manzanar internment camp for Japanese-Americans in Lone Pine, California, well knew the importance of *home.* A few Sundays after reading *Bokotola,* Jack distributed copies of the book to every person in his congregation, the Almaden Valley United Church of Christ in San Jose, and preached a spellbinding sermon challenging them to do something about this great need.

At that time there were no Habitat affiliates in California. But the folks in San Jose decided to think *big.* (They were undoubtedly encouraged in this respect by a big church member who was one of Jack's first recruits to the cause. Dave Eastis, along with his whole family, quickly became a stalwart Habitat partner. A former college basketball player who stands 6'7" and weighs two hundred and fifty pounds, Dave likes to look down at me. I'm three inches shorter. Dave and I have become fast friends, despite the fact that he persists in calling me "the skinny kid.")

The Almaden Valley Church formed Habitat West, an organization devoted entirely to promoting the Habitat concept wherever they could get a group to listen. They began speaking and fundraising throughout central California, and volunteers and contributions to build houses overseas began arriving regularly in Americus.

Eight years later, in the spring of 1986, there were six Habitat projects in California. One of these was in Fresno, which had become Habitat's one hundredth affiliate the year before. A prime mover of the Fresno effort was Rev. Jack Takayanagi, who was by that time pastoring the College Community Congregational Church there, and whose vision for providing shelter for people in need absolutely knows no bounds.

In 1983, the president of Habitat West, Jim Carr, was contacted by another Habitat supporter I had discovered in Chicago, who happened to have the same name. The man from the Windy City flew out to meet his California counterpart. Before long, Habitat Midwest, covering nine states, was being formed in Chicago. The new president: Jim Carr!

In other parts of the United States, Habitat partners have been inspired to form similar organizations, which we now call Regional Centers.[1] Each Regional Center covers several states and offers speakers, guidance, and resources of all kinds to Habitat affiliates and other interested groups in their geographical areas. They also vigorously promote and encourage support for the worldwide work of Habitat for Humanity. And in every case a few people, impelled by a profound spiritual motivation, have made the difference.

In Acton, Massachusetts, Ron and Barbara Yates, fired up after a big Habitat meeting in the Midwest, were led to form Habitat Northeast in the fall of 1983. Since that time, both have devoted enormous energy to this effort throughout New England and New York—and they have never wearied in well-doing. In fact, says Barbara, "Our involvement in Habitat has been a wonderful gift to both of us."

Out in Springfield, Missouri, Keith and Karen Jaspers and their daughter Kelly were also getting caught up in the vision. And after a two-week work trip to the Habitat project in Haiti, they were totally committed. The Jaspers soon found that the Lord was enabling them to recruit a wealth of assistance from diverse denominations in a community, Keith told us, "normally divided by personal interests, pride, and local church projects." By 1986, Habitat of the Ozarks, a Regional Center headquartered in Springfield, was providing leadership to projects in three states, and at the same time it was generating enough money, through imaginative fundraising, to build two overseas houses per month!

Mary Elizabeth and Mason Schumacher in Boulder, Colorado, cheerfully took on another vast area. Following visits to Habitat projects in Peru and in Americus, the Schumachers inaugurated Rocky Mountain Habitat, a Regional Center for four states covering an area of 404,000 square miles. Distances between projects out there are great—but so are the hearts of these Habitat visionaries.

Mary Brock, of Dallas, Texas, attended her first Habitat meeting in November of 1985. Mary was an experienced organizer seeking a fresh challenge, and Habitat was glad to supply one. Within four months she had convened a gathering which resulted in the formation of Habitat Southwest, covering the huge territory of Texas and Oklahoma.

In December of 1985, the brand new Habitat affiliate in Jersey City, New Jersey, received a large Christmas gift—the deed to an abandoned building on the dismal corner of Bergen Avenue and Grant Street, in the midst of what President Skip Dolan referred to as a "war zone." The small Habitat committee took possession of a boarded-up five-story brick edifice which originally held forty-seven apartment units. Although a five-hundred-home Habitat development was currently underway astride the equator near Mbandaka, Zaire, this renovation in Jersey City would be the largest U.S. undertaking in Habitat's history.

Confident of the Lord's leading, the committee plunged in. They enlisted the support of the mayor, the city council, and the district's congressman. Area newspapers, both English and Spanish, the Board of Education, the Private Industry Council, local realtors, and trade unions all pitched in to help. By February of 1986, more than one hundred families had already filed applications, and Jersey City Habitat's goal was to have most of the apartments rehabilitated and occupied within one year. With their faith and determination, I'm betting they'll make it.

We *can* get everybody properly housed. Everywhere. We *can* get rid of the shacks. The problem we face is not too large for the Lord.

The year 1987 has been designated by the United Nations General Assembly as the International Year of Shelter for the Homeless. The introduction to a booklet explaining this program includes these words: "It is imperative that a focused and coordinated worldwide effort be launched—*now.*"

We in Habitat for Humanity couldn't agree more.

The statistics I've gathered here are mind-boggling, and the size of the problem is awesome. But it is not insoluble. There is a terrible temptation to attend to our own comfort only, and to turn our backs on the needs of others. When we do that, *we* become part of the problem.

Let's find ways to become part of the solution.

---

1. See Appendix C for a list of these locations.

5

"Linda, Let's
Take a Walk."

The air was windy and chilly. An overcast sky glowered, and it looked as though rain might begin at any moment.

I stood in the front doorway of our home in Americus, Georgia, on a Sunday afternoon in early April of 1983. For several weeks I had been thinking about walking from Americus to Indianapolis, a distance of seven hundred miles. On the third weekend of September, a grand celebration for Habitat's seventh birthday was planned in Indianapolis in conjunction with the fall board meeting. It had occurred to me that walking to this event would help dramatize the need for housing, and sensitize more people to the big problem we were trying to solve.

I hadn't even told Linda what was on my mind. The idea seemed preposterous, but it wouldn't go away. I wondered if I *could* walk that far. I felt I was in good physical condition, but I had never tried anything like a seven-hundred-mile walk!

At the moment, I had a more modest goal in mind. I was contemplating an eight-mile walk to Koinonia Farm to attend the Sunday afternoon worship service. I wanted to see how I felt after doing that. The service started at four o'clock; it was already nearly two. I hesitated. The weather looked forbidding. But I knew that I must decide one way or the other now, because it would take at least two hours to walk to Koinonia.

I decided to go. Rushing back into the house, I blurted out to Linda, "I'm going to the service at Koinonia, and I'm walking."

"You're what?"

"I'm walking."

"Why? It looks like rain. Why in the world are you *walking* out there?"

"I'll tell you later. You're coming out, aren't you?"

"Yes, I was planning to."

"Good. I'll ride back with you. See you there."

I grabbed a cap and an umbrella, and bolted out the door.

I walked at a brisk pace. I wanted to get to Koinonia in time for the service, and the clouds did look ominous. After about four miles the rain started in earnest, and the wind began to blow right in my face. Walking became much more difficult, but I trudged on. At a quarter after four, drenched and totally exhausted, I turned into the driveway at the farm. Instead of going directly to the service, which was already in progress, I stopped at the first house to rest and catch my breath. As I sat down I noticed that my legs were shaking. I thought to myself, "I've walked only eight miles, and I'm in this condition. It's a good thing I haven't announced that I'm thinking about walking seven hundred miles. People would really laugh!"

Within a few minutes I had recovered enough to go on to the service. The next day I was sore, but not as miserably as I'd expected. I began to feel that I had crossed the threshold. The walk to Koinonia settled it. I would walk to Indianapolis.

On the way home after the Sunday service, Linda and I had talked about the walk. The idea intrigued her. She was interested in walking too, but not in going the whole distance. She and I, alternating, could *possibly* go the whole way, she thought. She would walk for three or four hours while I rode in a support vehicle.

Then she would ride while I walked. Trying to walk the whole way was too much. Linda was adamant. She would eventually change her mind, but not today!

I had earlier discussed the possibility of such a walk with a special "Committee of Seven"[1] which had been formed to help raise an extra million dollars in connection with the Indianapolis Habitat Celebration. We simply had to come up with some dramatic new ways to call attention to the problem of deplorable housing in our world. And then we had to inspire fresh support for solving that problem.

After the committee had put forth a variety of ideas on how to generate a million dollars, I suggested that I might organize a walk from Americus to Indianapolis. It could be promoted in the Habitat newsletter, and people could be asked to make pledges of so much a mile. I would also urge others to join me on the walk, either for the whole distance or some part of it. They too would get pledges. We could set a goal of raising a hundred thousand dollars. That would be a tenth of the million-dollar goal.

The committee's initial reaction to the idea was stunned silence. Some members questioned the wisdom of such an effort. "Wouldn't that take too much time away from your busy schedule?" "What about the danger in walking along the edge of the highway?" "Would the walk come across as a gimmick?"

Others thought perhaps the walk was a good suggestion, but there was certainly no great enthusiasm for it immediately. As we continued to talk, however, the proposal seemed to make more and more sense. The committee's conclusion was simply that I should think and pray about the matter and then make the final decision.

The rainy walk to Koinonia closed the final link in my chain of thoughts and prayers on the subject. I would go, and I was really pleased that Linda wanted to go, too.

Plans for the celebration itself had been under way for a year. Habitat for Humanity would be seven years old as an organization in September 1983. Seven is an important Biblical number signifying holiness, completion, and rest. Why not a big meeting calling everyone together to rejoice? Habitat was experiencing tremendous growth, and we thought it entirely appropriate to celebrate what had been accomplished and to give the work a jolt of inspiration to propel us onward. Outstanding Christian leaders from Zaire, Uganda, Peru, and other countries would be there to tell us about the plight of their poorly housed people, and to challenge us to move boldly ahead to meet the need in the name of Christ. Speakers from throughout the United States would also share their encouragement, telling of needs in our own country, and what Habitat was doing to answer them. We would even have a parade with banners and balloons! Over a thousand supporters were expected to attend, in the largest Habitat gathering ever.

We knew, of course, that the gathering would attract valuable notice from the media; the walk would draw even more attention to the work of Habitat. I announced the walk in a memo to Habitat directors and advisors as soon as our decision was definite. We would leave Americus on August 3, planning to arrive in Indianapolis on September 13. We also invited local Habitat volunteers and friends to join us.

The first person to announce he would walk with us was Hugh O'Brien from Bailieboro, Ireland. Hugh, a robust sixty-six-year-old bachelor, first showed up in Americus in September of 1982. He had traveled by bus from the Yukon, where he had been doing volunteer carpentry work with a Catholic priest, helping to complete a church building. Someone in Canada had given him a copy of *Love in the Mortar Joints*. The book had inspired Hugh to get on a bus and come down to Georgia to see if what he had read about was really happening.

A policeman announced Hugh's arrival with a phone call to my home at 3:00 A.M.

"Mr. Fuller, a man is standing outside Habitat headquarters who wants to see you."

"At three o'clock in the morning?"

"Yes. He says he came here from the Yukon."

"I'll be right down." We don't get many visitors from the Yukon!

I liked Hugh the moment I met him. Small and totally bald, Hugh had only a few teeth visible when a grin split his square face. His outfit consisted of a baggy shirt and trousers (the latter held up by broad suspenders), topped by a flat floppy cap. We soon learned his garb was the same for all occasions.

Hugh was a man with a mission. For years he had been going out to places like Ontario and the Yukon and India simply to help people. He was a one-person Irish Christian Peace Corps. A persistent and hard worker, Hugh knew construction. He also knew how to live on practically nothing. Once, he said, he arrived in New York with twenty dollars, stayed for several months, and returned home with most of his money!

Hugh volunteered for the Habitat construction crew in Americus on the day of his arrival, and served faithfully for some months. As soon as he heard about the walk he determined to go. In Americus, he walked or rode a bicycle everywhere, and I did not doubt that he could walk to Indianapolis.

Gradually others began to sign on with us, for all or part of the distance.

Sam Lott, an Americus businessman, would walk one hundred and forty miles, to Atlanta. He hoped to raise fifteen thousand dollars to build a house for one local family.

Ann Nettum, another Americus friend, would meet us in Atlanta and walk from there.

Dan Rhema, former director of Baltimore Habitat, was now in orientation in Americus with his wife, Susan, preparing for service in Kenya. He would walk as far as Atlanta. An experienced distance walker, Dan provided all of us with valuable advice on training.

Sally Winter, a nurse from Akron, Ohio, visited Americus in July, learned that we'd been praying for a nurse to accompany us, and said, "I'll go!"

Mark Frey, then director of Appalachia Habitat for Humanity, and *Bill Underhill*, a seventy-five-year-old volunteer in that project, would walk with us across Tennessee.

Zenon Colque Rojas, director of the Puno, Peru, Habitat project, sent word that he would walk the whole distance.

Dan Roman, from Mesa, Arizona, was just completing two years as a Habitat volunteer in Zaire, and as soon as he got home in August, he would join us.

Our daughter *Faith*, sixteen, and another local teenager, *Andrew*

Bates, fourteen, would walk as far as Atlanta, then they would have to return to start school.

Sandra Graham, a longtime Habitat supporter from Easley, South Carolina, would join us for the last fifty miles in Indiana.

In late April, Linda and I began to go out in the afternoons to get in shape, walking three miles or more each time. One favorite route was a circuit of the town measuring 5.6 miles. On other occasions we would walk to the half-mile "jogging circle" in a lovely grove of pine trees at nearby Georgia Southwestern College, run around it a few times and walk back home. Linda also started a regular program of swimming and aerobic exercises.

As we got stronger from our training, we increased the tempo and the distance. We would get someone to drive us ten to fifteen miles out various roads leading into Americus, and then we'd walk back. We found ourselves exploring interesting byways: the Hooks Mill Road, the Middle River Road, the Bumphead Road, the Andersonville Road, the Plains Road.

Eventually Linda began to feel that she could go the full seven hundred miles. She felt I could, too. The "alternating" idea was dropped. We would walk together the whole way, from Americus to Indianapolis.

The week prior to our departure date of August 3, we walked fifteen miles on each of two consecutive days and ten miles on the third day. We felt good following this sustained period of walking, so we believed we were ready for the main event.

We had announced our plans in the June-July issue of the Habitat newsletter, spelling out the three-fold purpose of the walk:

> First of all, as concerned Christians, we want to dramatize the need of *so many* people in our world for a simple, decent place in which to live. We want to call attention to the urgency of this problem and to make a bold statement that the problem, as enormous as it is, *can be solved*. Jesus tells us that with God, all things are possible, and we believe it! However, God has no hands but ours and no feet but ours. . . .
>
> Second, we hope to raise at least a hundred thousand dollars by this walk. We are calling on people to make pledges of so much a mile, to be paid before the end of 1983. . . .

The third purpose of our long trek is simply to say to you that if we can walk from Americus, you should be able to get to Indianapolis somehow! Perhaps you'd like to walk with us. Write if you're interested. You can walk the whole distance, or some part of it.

On July 16, we held a dedication service in Americus for the newly renovated house of Bessie Moore. At that service, her twelve-year-old son Henry told me he would like to go on the walk. He wanted to go the whole distance, but the start of school would prevent that. I talked the matter over with his mother, and she agreed that he could go as far as Atlanta. He had never been there. His family had no car and rarely went anywhere outside the town of Americus.

Henry immediately started walking with Linda and me, along with others who were training for the walk. And he began signing people up for pledges. By the time we left on the walk, he had signed up practically his entire neighborhood. His total pledges exceeded $2,000!

One day when we were practice-walking from Andersonville to Americus, I asked Henry what he liked best about his new house. Without hesitation he replied, "My own room." Before the renovations, Henry, his sister, and his mother all slept in one small room.

Then I asked Henry why he wanted to go on the walk. He thought for a minute and then answered softly, "I want to help other people get a good house, too."

As our departure date neared, excitement continued to build. A week before we left, Cecil Miller, a young retiree from New Paris, Indiana, arrived in Americus with his camper. Cecil had volunteered to go with us to cook meals, transport sleeping bags, and supply general logistical support. His wife Jeanette would join us in northern Kentucky. Wallace and Nancy Braud and Claire Williams, volunteers from the Americus office, had already driven the entire route, taking extensive notes about landmarks and towns along the way, and making arrangements with churches where we could sleep.

Gifts and pledges were coming in. We had reached nearly half of our goal before we even started on the walk. The most exciting pledge arrived on the morning of July 4. I was standing in the kitchen with Linda when the phone rang.

"Millard, this is Jim Handley."

"Hello, Jim!"

Jim and Ginny Handley were special Habitat friends from Harbor Beach, Michigan. In 1982, when I was planning a trip to Papua New Guinea and on around the world to visit potential Habitat project sites and existing projects, the Handleys donated money so Linda could accompany me. When the campaign was announced to raise the extra million dollars in connection with the celebration, they gave a generous donation. Now, Jim had some more good news.

"Millard, we have just received your June-July newsletter announcing your walk to Indianapolis. We think that is fantastic. Ginny and I want to give $20,000 toward your goal!"

I just about dropped the phone. "Jim, that is tremendous. Thank you! Thank you!"

Shortly before we left Americus, the Habitat office staff presented to Linda and me a giant pledge card, showing pledges totaling forty-four cents a mile, and a cake with the words "Indy 700 Walk" inscribed across the top.

On the night before we left, Linda and I were making final preparations when the phone rang. It was Rosalynn Carter's secretary, informing us that Rosalynn and her daughter, Amy, would join us the next morning for the sendoff, and would walk with us to the edge of town.

At 6:00 A.M. on Wednesday, August 3, 1983, a large crowd gathered in front of the Habitat office on West Church Street. We held a brief farewell ceremony, which closed with shouts of "Habitat Oyée!" This was a cheer we had brought home from Zaire. If you hold a big meeting there, and you want to affirm someone or something, the leader simply yells the name, followed by "Oyée!" (pronounced OH-YEA) and the crowd echoes, "Oyée!" It's a great way to boost enthusiasm.

At 6:30 the entire assemblage fell in behind a banner reading:

700 MILE WALK
AMERICUS TO INDIANAPOLIS
HABITAT FOR HUMANITY

For these first few blocks, we were over two hundred strong. We marched up Dudley Street, past the Court House, turned right on Lamar Street, and headed into downtown Americus singing lustily, "We're Marching to Zion."

I was overflowing with conflicting emotions. This old hymn had tremendous significance for Linda and me. It was the song God put in our hearts eighteen years earlier, when we were returning to Alabama on a plane from New York City. We had just decided to change our lives' direction completely, and to follow a path of Christian service.

I was emotional for other reasons, too. Nearly fourteen years earlier, on October 29, 1969, I had driven a Chevrolet station wagon slowly up this same street with the sheet-draped body of Clarence Jordan in the back. After he had died suddenly while working in his "writing shack" at Koinonia, I had called the coroner to come out to examine the body. He wouldn't come. The medical examiner wouldn't come, either. Clarence was hated in Americus and Sumter County because he championed the cause of black people, and because he led what local folks called "that integrated communist community." So I had to drive his body to the hospital for an autopsy in order to get a death certificate before he could be buried back on the farm he loved.

I remembered also the last time I had led a walk up this street. It was in August 1971, and the black citizens of Americus had become incensed over instances of police brutality. Meetings were being held in black churches all over town. Protest walks were being staged around the court house. Several of us from Koinonia, after investigating the citizens' complaints, had joined their cause, and hundreds of people had marched along this same route singing "We Shall Overcome" and "Ain't Nobody Gonna Turn Us Around."

Since then, times had changed remarkably. Today we walked, not a crowd of blacks with a few whites, protesting what whites were doing to blacks, but a totally integrated group, and the mayor, the police chief, a former first lady, and a black city councilman were with us, on the way to celebrate what we had been doing together to help one another. It was a joyous experience.

We turned left at James Chevrolet and headed north on Lee Street. On my left I saw the building that was once Birdsie's Feed Store. It had been dynamited in the late fifties because the store sold some things to Koinonia during the boycott by local merchants. It was never reopened. Now, however, every other store in town was gladly doing business with the farm.

On up North Lee Street we marched, singing, shouting, and yelling, "Habitat Oyée!" We passed a long row of trim houses on the left and a couple more on the right, all built by the Partnership Housing program of Koinonia. Ahead of us and to the right, strung out on the other side of Price Street, was another long row of neatly kept houses, all built by Koinonia, using biblical economics. Twenty-three new homes had been built right around the middle school on this corner by Koinonia and Habitat building crews, replacing the falling-down shacks that had stood there a few years earlier.

As my eye scanned these sturdy homes, and as many of the occupants stood in their yards and waved to us, my heart filled up again with emotion, and I could feel tears coming. "This is why we're walking," I thought.

As we turned left onto Patterson Street, heading for Highway 19 to Atlanta, the housing scene changed. Along here, some better housing was mixed with many shacks—a vivid reminder that our job was far from complete. Those sad structures gave urgent meaning to our walk.

"There's Highway 19! Everybody turn right! As we come onto the highway, everybody sing!"

> Come, we that love the Lord,
> And let our joys be known,
> Join in a song with sweet accord,
> Join in a song with sweet accord,
> And thus surround the throne,
> And thus surround the throne.
>
> We're marching to Zion,
> Beautiful, beautiful Zion;
> We're marching upward to Zion,
> The beautiful city of God.[2]

A police escort was leading us, so we just took over the highway for the next couple of miles. Cars were backed up for hundreds of yards before we gave the road back to them at Markette's Nursery, just north of the Americus city limits.

At that point most of the people turned back. Our oldest daughter, Kim, had walked that far with us. She gave Linda and me a big hug. We hugged a lot of other people, too. Then, amid vigorous waving and a few more "Oyées," we headed north.

We had scheduled ten days for the walk to Atlanta. That was a little slower pace than we could have gone, but this was a new experience for all of us. We decided to be conservative on the first segment. It was midsummer in Georgia, so we usually walked from a little before daybreak until noon. At about ten each morning, Cecil Miller would catch up with us in his camper, bearing gifts of fruit, iced tea, and cookies. He was always a welcome sight, not only for his goodies, but also for his delightful sense of humor and his encouragement.

Each walker carried a day pack with a canteen of water, a sack of trail mix, and an extra pair of socks. After lunch, we would rest. Sometimes, if the day cooled late in the afternoon, we would walk some more.

On Saturday morning, August 6, we crossed the Flint River, which is supposed to be the "gnat line." South of the river, there are millions of little black insects that love to fly into your eyes, nose, and mouth from early summer until frost. North of the Flint River, however, you seldom see the pesky little critters. Needless to say, we were glad to cross that body of water!

Just south of Thomaston, two carloads of workcampers from First Baptist Church in Clemson, South Carolina, drove up and got out to walk with us. They had been working in Americus for the past week and were now returning home. Tom Hall, from the Habitat office, and his wife, Dianne, also drove up about the same time with their three children. They would join us for the walk through the city of Thomaston.

Vickie Lott, Sam's wife, had been traveling with us for a couple of days, serving as a promoter for the walk. She would go ahead of us into the next town and arrange for media interviews and meetings with church and civic leaders. In Thomaston, where the Clemson work campers joined us, she had arranged something special. A police escort met us at the southern edge of town to lead us through the city. I herded together our suddenly enlarged group.

"Come on, everybody! We'll walk briskly behind the police car. Pass out Habitat materials to anyone who seems interested. Let's go!"

Right through the middle of town we marched, yelling, "Habitat Oyée!" and poking Habitat newsletters and fliers into the windows of every car that had a driver with a friendly face, and into the hands of anyone on the sidewalks who looked receptive. The policeman kept sounding his siren every couple of minutes, so no one could ignore us.

On the north side of town, we stopped at a McDonald's where Vickie had arranged for us to have a free lunch. While we were eating, we were surprised to see Amy Carter come in. At that point I was being interviewed by a *Thomaston Times* reporter. She decided a picture of me with Amy would be nice, and asked us to stand together. Then she spent considerable time aiming her camera, repeatedly holding it sideways and then up and down.

Finally she exclaimed in dismay, "I just can't take this picture, because Millard is so much taller than Amy!"

Amy, who is 5'3", shot back, "I can solve that." She stretched up on her tiptoes, I scrunched my 6'4" frame a bit, and the reporter snapped our picture.

That afternoon I taped an interview with a local radio station, to be used on their evening news. At suppertime, all of the walkers were together in the fellowship hall of the Presbyterian church listening to the broadcast. The station used the first part of the interview, then it was abruptly cut off to insert a commercial for a local savings and loan association. The sudden transition from my talking about housing for the poor at no profit and no interest to the savings and loan's sales pitch to the affluent was so startling that everyone roared with laughter.

We stayed overnight in Thomaston in homes of various church families. On Sunday morning we fanned out to different churches in the city to worship and to tell the Habitat story; in the afternoon we walked northward toward the little town of Zebulon.

Just south of the city limits of Zebulon, a group of campers from First Baptist Church in Thomaston caught up with us. There were fifty of them, ages eight to sixteen, in a big bus. Some of our walkers had attended church at First Baptist, so the campers knew about the walk, and they wanted to join us for a while. I got on the bus and told them more about Habitat and specifically what the walk was about. Then I taught them how to yell "Habitat Oyée!" The young people got into that routine quickly, so we stormed through Zebulon, over sixty of us, yelling, "Habitat Oyée! Indianapolis Oyée! Good houses Oyée!" Then the bus went on, and we stopped for the night.

In Zebulon, our campsite was the expansive yard of Dr. Evelyn Berry and her sister, Dorothy Dunn. They lived on top of a lovely hill, adjacent to the town's golf course. We set up our tents and enjoyed wandering around the grounds, taking cold showers with a hose, and finding no gnats!

On Monday morning we walked north toward Griffin. A few miles out of Zebulon, a little grey-haired lady hurried out of her house.

"Are you Christians?" she asked.

"Praise the Lord—we sure are!"

"Well, I'm Annie Durden. Come over here and sit down," she said, motioning to some yard chairs. "I've got something for you."

She returned to the house and emerged with a beautiful strawberry cake and a jug of ice water. We sat visiting with her for half an hour. Before we left, all the cake was gone as well as refills on the ice water. We felt delightfully refreshed, not only by food and rest, but also by an unexpected encounter with a charming lady.

A few miles farther, we met an older man cutting his grass. He had heard of Habitat for Humanity and the walk, and then and there he made a pledge.

Shortly before noon we met a farmer along the road. He gave us a big sack of fresh cucumbers.

That night we stayed at Cornerstone Church, just south of Griffin. We walked in the door and made a welcome discovery: The

Sunday school department, where we would sleep, was air-conditioned!

The next day our goal was the Bonanza United Church of Christ in Jonesboro, twenty miles away. We started at 6:00 A.M. and walked until past noon. By eleven o'clock the heat was incredible. Faith had huge blisters on her right foot, so she had removed one shoe, and she hobbled down the road, grimacing with every step.

At the beginning of that day, Hugh O'Brien had stayed in front of the main body of walkers, but later he fell behind. Eventually he dropped out of sight entirely, and I became concerned. I asked Dan Rhema to wait for Hugh to catch up, and the rest of us continued. Finally we reached the Jonesboro church. Twenty minutes went by and still no Dan and Hugh. Thirty minutes. Forty-five minutes.

I asked Cecil to drive back with me to check on the two men. About a quarter of a mile away, we saw them trudging along. Hugh had found an old sheet somewhere along the road and had draped it over his head to cut off some of the sun's blistering rays. He looked just like a robed Klansman! Totally exhausted, as all of us were, they finally made it to the church.

Over the next couple of days, we walked the remaining twenty miles into Atlanta, enjoying other activities between our walking times. One afternoon we attended an Atlanta Braves baseball game, compliments of the Bonanza church. That was a real treat for Henry Moore, who had never attended a big league game.

On Friday, August 12, we walked up the front steps of the Georgia State Capital Building. Secretary of State Max Cleland was scheduled to present us with a proclamation from the governor concerning the walk, and at least a hundred people were gathered in the rotunda of the capital for the event. Newspaper and television reporters were on hand. But no Max Cleland. We waited and waited. The reporters were getting restless. So was everybody else. Finally, word came: The Secretary of State was locked in a huge traffic jam, and no one had any idea when he would arrive.

At this point an assistant appeared bearing the proclamation. Solemnly he began to read. Every time he came to my name in the text, he read it as "Mildred Fuller." At first there were snickers, and then great peals of laughter every time he read "Mildred." I don't think he ever figured out what he was saying to produce all those guffaws.

Mayor Andrew Young also had a representative present to read a proclamation from the city. August 12 was designated Habitat for Humanity Day in the city of Atlanta and throughout the state.

The next morning all of the walkers, plus new recruits Sally Winter and Ann Nettum (but minus those who had planned to walk only to Atlanta—Faith Fuller, Henry Moore, Sam Lott, and Dan Rhema), met at Trinity United Methodist Church to continue the walk northward. Several of the folks from the new Atlanta Habitat project met us there, too, and walked a couple of miles with us. Everyone was in high spirits. The walk from Americus to Atlanta had been a great experience. Over five hundred miles were still ahead of us, but we were ready.

It took us five days to walk to the Tennessee line. Along that stretch we were joined by volunteer Dan Roman, just back from Zaire. Dan would stay with the walk all the way to Indianapolis. He would also fall in love with Sally Winter somewhere between Georgia and Indiana, and marry her a year later!

In Dalton, Georgia, Solomon Maendel and his twelve-year-old son Mark arrived. Solomon, from the Forest River Hutterite Colony near Fordville, North Dakota, was driving a station wagon which had been lent to him for the walk by a businessman in his area. It was loaded with sunflower seeds, honey, eggs, and summer sausage, all from the Colony farm. Solomon, a longtime friend of Habitat for Humanity who, with his family, had worked as a volunteer for several months in Americus, would remain with us the rest of the way to Indianapolis, doing the kind of promotional work Vickie Lott had done from Americus to Atlanta.

Just south of the Tennessee border, our son, Chris, drove up with Habitat's Media Director Wallace Braud, who had come to shoot some footage of the walk. Chris had been working in Saudi Arabia all summer. He would stay with us only for a day, but it was a real boost to see him.

As we approached the Tennessee line, we unfurled our banner from the camper and began to sing "We're Marching to Zion." Mark Frey was waiting at the border, along with Appalachia volunteers Bill and Ruth Underhill, other Habitat people, and half a dozen media folks. The Appalachia Habitat supporters had their own banner. A great roar of welcome went up as we stepped over into Tennessee.

We headed straight for Chattanooga, nine miles away, with the sun beating down overhead and a temperature of well over a hundred degrees. In downtown Chattanooga we encountered a waterfall in a public park, and within moments everyone was happily soaked.

The next day we walked steadily northward, crossing the Sequatchie River, passing through Dunlap, Pikeville, and into Crossville.

It was Monday morning, August 22, when Frank Basler of North Carolina, a longtime Habitat partner, arrived to walk with us for a day. He had chosen the hottest one of the entire pilgrimage. When we turned into the driveway of the Shady Veil Church of God just south of Crossville for lunch, all of us were drenched in perspiration, and the thermometer read 110 degrees.

Crossville was the halfway point of the walk. When Frank Basler learned that he exclaimed, "Well, that calls for a celebration!" He gave us $100 and told us to live it up. So that evening, we did. We all devoured a big meal at a lakeside restaurant in Cumberland State Park. It cost us $66. That still left $34 to apply toward our $100,000 goal!

The first night in the Crossville area, we were hosted by Cumberland Homestead Baptist Church, which is located across from the entrance to the Cumberland State Park. As we were settling in at the church fellowship hall, the pastor and his wife, Houston and Sherlene Inman, came in. I started playing my harmonica. Houston fetched his guitar. Within a few minutes, everyone was singing.

The evening began to fly. Dan Roman shared a song in Lingala, the language of the people where he had been working in Zaire. Ann Nettum and I sang a duet. Linda and I sang another. Hugh O'Brien belted out an Irish folk song. Ann, Sally, and Dan offered a song they had composed especially for that evening. We got out hymn books and sang some more, one old favorite after another, for hours. Zenon Colque Rojas, a Roman Catholic Peruvian who was just learning English, had no familiarity with any of the music, but he joined in as enthusiastically as any of us. Suddenly it was midnight, and everyone was amazed. When we realized that the experience of such great fellowship was coming to an end, everyone just looked at each other; tears of rejoicing came to our eyes.

We all stood in a circle and held hands while Houston led us in prayer. He poured out his heart in thanksgiving for that special evening. Then both he and Sherlene expressed profound gratitude to us. They said we had come at a low point in their lives. He had been a lifelong chaplain in Tennessee prisons and had lost that job the previous year; they had felt lonely since coming to this church, and Sherlene, who was a career teacher, had not found work. Both of them had been deeply discouraged. For us, there was unspeakable joy in learning that the Lord had used us to bring encouragement to these folks. And all the while we were having such a wonderful time!

The next day we continued our walk into downtown Crossville. Linda and Sally were experiencing real trouble with blisters. Every few hours they were having to lance the blisters, bandage them up and trudge on. By the time the trip was over, they had gone through fifteen economy size boxes of Band-aids, several packages of cotton (for stuffing between toes), and a dozen boxes of moleskin.

I began to take note of the interesting signs in front of Tennessee churches. One admonished, "Jealousy is a horse which the devil likes to ride." Another read, "Sorrow looks back; worry looks around; faith looks up." The names of the churches were interesting, too. We saw the Rinnie Baptist Church, the New Charity Separate Baptist Church, Isoline Missionary Baptist Church, Coffey's Friendship Separate Baptist Church, the Church of God of Prophesy, and Faith Baptist Church, Independent, Fundamental, Premillenial. All the notable names were not on churches, either. We also passed the Bushwacker Beauty Shop, the Dead Rat Tavern, and the Fat Rat Saloon!

On Friday, August 26, we made a detour east by car so we could walk through Morgan and Scott counties, site of the Appalachia Habitat project. At Barton's Chapel in Robbins, where Mark Frey was pastor, we shared a luncheon. Then we walked north again.

At 7:30 that evening we crossed Perkins Creek, about half a mile south of the Kentucky state line. Just past the creek was the Wooden Nickel, some sort of night club, and lining the road on both sides from there to the border was a wild conglomeration of taverns, saloons, and beer joints. The section of Kentucky we were about to enter was dry, so citizens thirsty for alcohol had to drive into Tennessee to get tanked up. At exactly 8:00 P.M. we crossed into Kentucky, dead tired but singing at the top of our voices, "We're Marching to Zion!"

The next day, we continued north on U.S. 27 through the Daniel Boone National Forest. The narrow road wound up a steep hillside, and by noon we had reached a little grocery store at the top. Giant trees surrounded us. A sign above the store entrance read, "U.S. Post Office—Wiborg, Kentucky." We were now fifteen miles beyond Tennessee. After a lunch of junk food from the store, we walked another four miles and called it a day.

The next morning, Solomon drove us west to our main route to Indianapolis, Highway 127. At another point nineteen miles north of the Tennessee-Kentucky border he let us out. We were now six: Linda, Zenon, Dan, Sally, Hugh, and I; Ann had had to return to Americus the day before.

We climbed out of the car, scanning an overcast sky. We wondered if Solomon should stay with us in case of rain. As if in reply, there was a loud drum roll of thunder. Solomon beamed and exclaimed, "The Lord is speaking to you!"

It hadn't rained on us a single day so far. We decided to press on, and Solomon drove off ahead. Soon the rain started, but it was surprisingly light and lasted only a few minutes. That little sprinkle was all the rain we experienced on the entire walk. It frequently rained ahead of us, to either side of us, behind us, while we were resting in a building, or at night while we slept, but never on us while we were walking.

All through Kentucky we were surrounded by incredible beauty. The weather was cooler in the mountains, and occasionally we noticed that leaves were beginning to turn. In some places, the vistas were breathtaking. I tried to record some of them as we walked along.

We crossed the Wolf Creek Dam. The scenery is fantastic. Cedar trees grow right out of the rock cliffs along the road. Cumberland Lake is startlingly beautiful. A plaque reports that its shoreline is over twelve hundred miles.

Each morning we were walking in the dark, often by moonlight. Some of the scenes which are still indelibly printed in my memory took place just at daybreak.

The sun is rising. We cannot see it yet, but it is shining on the underside of the clouds on the eastern horizon, giving them a brilliant pink hue. The tops of the clouds are completely dark. There is practically no wind; the clouds scattered all over the sky above us appear not to move at all. . . . . At this moment we are traveling almost due east, so the sun is coming up right in front of us. It is a fiery orange ball with black mountains in the foreground.

Sometimes we saw things that were not so beautiful, but we rejoiced anyway. One day, on the southern outskirts of Columbia, we passed a deserted church. Ivy grew over the left side of the building, covering one of the front doors. To the right of the main structure was what looked like a Sunday school building. The windows were broken out and weeds surrounded everything. The church sign was old and warped, its paint peeling badly. On the highway right in front of the church lay a big opossum that had been crushed by some passing motorist. Its teeth glistened from underneath rotting flesh. The six of us were together as we walked by. We surveyed the whole scene, looked at each other, shivered a little, and spontaneously burst into "We're Marching to Zion!"

We often passed the time along the road watching for unusual cloud formations. One day Dan, Sally, and I studied a particularly interesting array, including an elephant with its trunk up in the air and a baby elephant tagging along behind, a camel looking back at us over his shoulder, an Eskimo igloo with two men running from the entrance, a mountain goat perched on a cliff, a turtle, a baboon, and two sea horses kissing each other!

Although the weather was generally cooler in Kentucky, there was one day in the southern part of the state that just about did us in. Cecil gave us our mid-morning snack and drove on, saying he would stop at a place where we could catch up to him around one o'clock. Unfortunately, there was no place for Cecil to pull over on the narrow road. He had to go much farther than he intended. We did not reach him until nearly three. By that time, the midday heat combined with twenty miles of continuous walking had nearly wiped us out. Furthermore, we were not encouraged by the fact that a collection of buzzards had been circling over us for nearly two hours!

When we finally saw Cecil, he had pulled over in the small village of Glen's Fork. Dan and Sally, who were a little behind the rest of us, dropped melodramatically to their knees and came slowly up to the camper that way, their faces contorted with mock expressions of great suffering.

To help us recover, Cecil served a terrific supper of tuna fish salad, tomatoes, fruit salad, baked potato, wheat bread, iced tea and chocolate chip cookies. A royal feast in a palace could not have been more eagerly received.

A couple of days later we found ourselves in front of Nazareth College, just north of Nazareth, Kentucky, at noon. Spotting some lovely trees at the entrance to the school, we walked over and were about to sit down when an official from the administration pulled up in a car.

"Are you in trouble?" she asked.

"Well, yes, we are," Solomon replied. "We're hungry and would like to eat in the shade."

"This is private property," she sternly informed us. "You can't eat here."

I told her we were with a Christian program called Habitat for Humanity, and that we were on a seven-hundred-mile walk to Indianapolis. We simply wanted to stop there for maybe thirty minutes for lunch.

"No," she insisted. "You can't eat here. We've had trouble with people getting on our property and bothering us, so we do not want you here." She did offer to find us a place off the road, but we explained that we needed to be by the highway because we were expecting a newspaper photographer to stop by and take some pictures. Then we left.

At the next house up the road, just off the college property, a young man was sitting on the porch drinking a can of beer. We yelled to him and asked if we could sit under the tree in his yard and eat our lunch.

"Sure," he called back. "Do you want to come in the house?"

"No, thank you," we told him. "We'll eat out here."

He promptly jumped up, ran around to the back yard and returned lugging a picnic table.

While we were eating, the young man's sister drove up. She was a student of nursing at a nearby university. When we told her about Habitat for Humanity and the walk, she became very excited. We gave her a Habitat T-shirt, and she immediately joined us for the next ten miles.

On Saturday, September 3, as we walked into Louisville, Rev. John Roemer, a United Church of Christ pastor in the city and a good friend of Habitat for Humanity, joined us. He had made a sign:

HABITAT FOR HUMANITY
BUILD HOUSES—NOT WEAPONS

Each of us took turns carrying it into town.

The next morning, Sunday, we split up and spoke in churches throughout the city. Linda spoke to a combined Sunday School class at the Douglass Boulevard Christian Church. I spoke at both morning worship services.

Cecil's wife, Jeanette, had arrived over the weekend. He was sure happy to see her, and they took a well-earned weekend off. Monday was Labor Day, so we all took the day off. I spent my time dictating a lot of tapes to be mailed back to the Habitat office in Americus for typing. All along the walk, sometimes as I was actually walking, I would dictate letters and memos to keep up with the correspondence from the office. This system worked just fine, and it kept me from falling hopelessly behind with my responsibilities back home.

On Tuesday morning we were back on the road again, ready to cross the Ohio River into Indiana. At the other end of the bridge, by prearrangement, we would be met and welcomed to the last state of our long trek by church and government officials and a group of special Habitat friends. We would also receive a proclamation from Robert Orr, governor of Indiana.

As we left the bridge and approached the appointed site for our meeting on the Indiana side, I was overjoyed to see so many familiar faces. We stopped walking long enough to exchange hugs, to listen to some short talks, and to receive the governor's proclamation. But Indianapolis was still a hundred and ten miles away. We were on the road again by ten o'clock.

Along this final segment, there were two evenings when Holiday Inns at Seymour and Columbus provided free motel rooms for all the walkers. We reveled in the unexpected luxury of hot showers, swimming pools, and Jacuzzis.®

On Monday morning, September 12, we gathered in the parking lot of St. John's United Church of Christ in Indianapolis. Roberts Park United Methodist Church, the site of the planned Habitat Celebration in the center of the city, was now just 8.1 miles away. As we traveled through Indiana we had gradually gathered more Habitat walkers, and there were now twenty-five in our group for the last lap.

Everyone was very emotional. The walk had been an unforgettable experience. We clasped hands in a large circle, offering prayers of thanksgiving for the walk and for our safe arrival.

About nine o'clock, we headed north toward the Roberts Park Church, singing energetically. We had acquired two new banners:

HABITAT FOR HUMANITY
SHELTER OF GOD'S LOVE
AMERICUS, GEORGIA

and

UNLESS THE LORD BUILDS THE HOUSE,
THOSE WHO BUILD IT LABOR IN VAIN.

The day was cloudy, which kept the temperature quite pleasant. Gene Crumley from Oregon, who had joined us several days back, spotted a dollar bill that was lying on the ground—the second one he had found. Everybody started yelling "Gene Oyée! Habitat Oyée!" All of us had picked up money along the way, and we were keeping it toward our $100,000 goal. Most of our finds were pennies, nickels, and dimes, but the total was now over five dollars. And from Americus we had learned that gifts and pledges sent in for the walk now exceeded $70,000.

At 10:30 A.M., Bishop Ogwal, president of the Habitat project in Gulu, Uganda, appeared. He had come to Indianapolis to be one of our keynote speakers at the celebration, and he fell in with us to walk the last couple of miles.

At eleven o'clock we saw the church. A crowd had gathered out front. Grover Hartman, chairman of the celebration, was beaming and holding a large bouquet of flowers sent by friends in Americus for Linda. Several media people were also present, but most important was the fact that *we were there!*

Over four hundred people had participated in some part of the walk. No one got hurt. There were blisters on top of blisters on top of still more blisters, but we made it, healthy and unbelievably happy. I think Linda and I were the happiest, though, when Grover handed me an envelope from our eleven-year-old daughter, Georgia. She had written a special poem for us:

> This very day I am proud to say
> That my mom and dad made it all the way!
> Not by car, bus, or jeep,
> But by their very own feet!
> I don't know how they did it,
> 'Cause I sure couldn't, I'll have to admit it.
> Gosh, two miles get me tired.
> Them walking all that way, I'll have to admire!
> I guess I was never made to walk long distances or run,
> But it sure sounds like a lot of fun!
> Mom and Dad, I just want to say,
> I LOVE YOU SO MUCH THIS VERY DAY!!!!

Georgia later read her poem to all the people at the celebration, but those lines were a tremendous gift to Linda and me as we arrived in Indianapolis after forty days on the road. We would never forget it.

Of course we would never forget the whole experience. We had been able to deliver the Habitat message in person to several thousand people along the way and expose thousands more to the work through extensive publicity. At least one new Habitat project would start as a direct result of the walk. And we would eventually reach our goal of $100,000. It had cost an enormous expenditure of time and energy, but all of us felt the effort was worthwhile. Most important of all, we had captured people's imaginations, calling attention to an overwhelming need. By any measure we might use, the walk had been a success.

The celebration that followed was spectacular. For three days Habitat folks from thirty-nine states, the District of Columbia, and twelve foreign countries jammed the Roberts Park Church.

One large meeting room contained wall-to-wall displays from Habitat projects everywhere. Artist Sharon Brown and her husband, Allan, of Parker City, Indiana, had arrived two days early to create this eye-catching exhibit.

Bishop Bokeleale, President of the Church of Christ of Zaire, spoke to our opening session on Thursday evening. He challenged us to continue with the urgent task of building for God's needy people. He also implored us to accelerate our work especially in his country, where poverty is so great.

On Friday, a succession of international church leaders addressed the meeting. After lunch, everyone marched to a beautiful park in the heart of the city. Project representatives carried colorful banners; the rest of us held helium-filled balloons. Clowns danced around us. We rejoiced and shouted our thanks to God.

For the big "Habitation" (a Habitat celebration) on Friday night, our media department had rushed to complete a slide show on the walk to Indianapolis, and the preponderance of sunburn-and-tired-feet photographs provided the assemblage with considerable amusement. Later the same evening, a slide presentation on home-building around the world titled "Celebrate Habitat" moved many viewers to tears.

On Saturday a special "separating out" service honored eight new volunteers who were about to leave for overseas projects. And David Rowe challenged us all with a spellbinding message on "Envisioning."

"It is not enough to speculate on social change. There are people who prefer to sit in a lovely office, talking and planning and theologizing. On the other extreme, there are terrorist groups who prefer to create mass horror and fear in the hope that some new order will emerge. But between the theory brokers and the terror brokers stand those like Habitat for Humanity, who choose to act, however humbly, who choose to serve, however inadequately, who choose to work, however meagerly. . . .

"So we build, and we build, and we build. We build houses, we build communities, we build friendships, we build mailing lists, we build compassion. We build with the spirit of God poured into every foundation, fired into every brick, driven into every board, turned in with every key. We build amid mountains of red tape, and frustration, and culture shock, and language difficulty, and personality conflicts, and financial crisis, and homesickness, and jealousy. But still somehow we squeeze the love of Jesus into every joint.

"And we don't build so that we can get into heaven. If you think so, leave now. We build because heaven is a glimpse of God's love. Our building is a symbol of how God's love and our love can work together. Heaven is a vision given to us by God to see us through difficult and dark days. Habitat is a vision given to us to put meaning into our work right now. . . ."

David's inspired words envisioned us all. We left Indianapolis fired up with fresh determination. And it was not long after this exciting weekend that I began thinking about walking the thousand miles from Americus to Kansas City for Habitat's tenth anniversary celebration in 1986.

But I didn't tell Linda about that right away.

---

1. Landrum Bolling—Washington, D.C.; David Eastis—San Jose, California; Keith Jaspers—Springfield, Missouri; Mary McCahon—New York, New York; Jim Millen—Akron, Pennsylvania; John Patton—Columbus, Ohio; John Pritchard—Kansas City, Missouri.
2. "Marching to Zion" by Isaac Watts and Robert Lowry.

6

A Presidential
Partner

"W e are pleased to have Millard Fuller with us today as our main speaker. Mr. Fuller works closely with former president Jimmy Carter, who founded Habitat for Humanity!"

The speaker was a city councilman in Tallahassee, Florida. He was introducing me at the August 1984 dedication service for a duplex house that had just been completed by Tallahassee Habitat for Humanity.

Obviously, the city councilman had heard some of the publicity about Jimmy Carter's involvement with Habitat, even though his facts were a little out of kilter, and now he was noticing what Habitat was doing in his own city. That's what was really important.

(Some people have said that I founded Habitat for Humanity. I know God was the founder. The idea came from heaven. It was first expressed on earth by Clarence Jordan, and by God's grace, I was privileged to be there to hear what the Lord said, through Clarence, back in 1968 and 1969. After Clarence left us for his eternal habitat in October 1969, I felt an unmistakable call to continue pursuing the dream. That call resulted in the formation of Habitat for Humanity in 1976.)

Every person who is involved in Habitat for Humanity in any way is important to this work. Every letter written, every slide show presented, and every contribution—physical labor, a shared idea, a can of paint, or a gift of money—is immensely important. And every house built, renovated, or repaired in any one of the scores of Habitat projects around the world is a significant part of the process of sensitizing, inspiring, and motivating people to get rid of the shacks and replace them with solid homes.

But when a former president of the United States joins forces with us, the resulting impetus is immeasurable. Suddenly Habitat for Humanity becomes known to millions of people. Credibility is established for the ministry, and new doors are opened to raising funds, securing volunteers, and acquiring land, tools, and materials.

Back in 1976, as Linda and I were winding up our three years of building houses for the poor in Zaire, Jimmy Carter was coming down the home stretch of a long campaign for the presidency of the United States. He won the election in November and began to prepare for four years in the White House. That same fall, Linda and I returned to Georgia and started working to establish Habitat for Humanity.

At that time we did not know Jimmy Carter. Once while he was in office, he attended a church service in Americus where our family was worshiping. We shook hands then and said maybe ten words to each other, but that was all.

President Carter first learned of Habitat for Humanity when his former neighbors in Plains, Ralph and Jane Gnann, decided to volunteer for two years with Habitat in Zaire. The Carters invited the Gnanns and their two sons to spend a couple of days with them in the White House shortly before the Gnanns left for Africa in September of 1980.

Of course President Carter had known of the work of Koinonia Farm for years, but he had never been directly involved in that ministry. He did share many ideals with the Koinonia Community.

But as an aspiring politician he knew, I'm sure, that to associate openly with Koinonia would have abruptly ended his career in public life. Koinonia was suspect as a "communist" organization, and any integrated group in South Georgia in the 1950s and 1960s was anathema to a majority of the white people.

After President Carter left the White House in January of 1981, he and Rosalynn moved back to their home in Plains. He had been a lifelong member of Plains Baptist Church, but that church had split during his time in Washington over the issue of openness to blacks. Members who felt that the church should welcome all races pulled out and built a smaller church about a mile down the road. The Carters joined the new congregation, called Maranatha Baptist, and President Carter became the teacher of the adult Sunday school class.

By this time, Habitat for Humanity had grown considerably, and more and more volunteers and work camps were coming to Americus. On Sundays, many of these people would attend Jimmy Carter's class, and from them he began to hear about the enlarging ministry of Habitat.

In 1982, as we were making plans for the fall meeting of Habitat's board of directors to be held in Americus in October, David Rowe suggested that we invite President Carter to bring greetings. I thought that was a super idea, but I had doubts about his willingness to come. I knew how incredibly busy he was. We felt that David, as board president, should issue the invitation. He told us later that he discarded a good many rough drafts before the final version of that letter was mailed to Plains. Shortly before our scheduled meetings in Americus, the Habitat office received a phone call. Our invitation had been accepted. Former president Jimmy Carter would come to the First Presbyterian Church on Saturday morning, October 16, 1982, to bring greetings and to speak briefly to our annual gathering of Habitat directors, advisors, and project representatives.

The sanctuary was packed when he arrived. As he entered the room, everyone rose, and there was long and enthusiastic applause.

The president began by discussing how difficult it is to put together theory and practical application in vital matters—human rights, stewardship of our resources, world peace. Habitat for Humanity, he said, is actually putting theory into practice in providing shelter for the poor. He emphasized his personal concern for the needs of refugees and the poor in Indochina, Haiti, and many other nations. Then he shared openly his feelings about Koinonia and Clarence Jordan.

"I am proud to be a neighbor of Koinonia . . . and to have seen, from perhaps too great a distance, the profound impact of Clarence Jordan on this country . . . and to have known this quiet man who demonstrated in his own life an image of Christ . . . with human fallibility, yes, but with the inspiration of Christ. I think I will be a better Christian because of Clarence Jordan, Koinonia, and Habitat. And I hope to grow the rest of my life, along with you."

Mr. Carter spoke for about ten minutes. He couldn't talk too long, he said, because he had to go home and study his Sunday school lesson. When the laughter subsided, he invited us all to worship at Maranatha Baptist Church the next day.

As he stepped from the pulpit, everyone jumped to their feet again and the sanctuary erupted in thunderous applause. There was universal appreciation for his presence and for his words of encouragement. And I believe he was impressed as well with the obvious concern and commitment of the Habitat folks.

Later in 1982, Habitat received a generous gift from President and Mrs. Carter. In August of the following year, the Carter family's personal involvement was enlarged when Rosalynn and Amy walked with us on the first morning of our long trek to Indianapolis. As we marched with a couple of hundred people through Americus to the city limits, I was able to talk to Rosalynn in some depth, not only about the walk, but also about the overall work of Habitat for Humanity. She seemed genuinely interested.

In December 1983, when we were ready to dedicate our expanded office building in Americus (we had taken the roof off the old house which served as our main office building and added a second story), we invited both President and Mrs. Carter to speak. They accepted, and they brought glowing words of affirmation to the two hundred and fifty people who attended.

That evening, I told Linda I was beginning to feel that the Carters really were interested in Habitat for Humanity. A couple of weeks later I called Faye Dill, President Carter's secretary in Plains, and asked for an appointment. She called me back with word that President Carter would see me on January 23, 1984, at ten in the morning.

On the appointed day, I drove the nine miles from Americus to Plains. I stopped at President Carter's office, which is located in his mother's former residence, a plain red-brick house on the south side of U.S. Highway 280, just a few dozen yards beyond the small Plains business district. There I was given clearance to pass through the security entrance to the Carters' home. I drove a short distance farther west on the same highway and turned right. The gate swung open and I passed through, drove thirty yards or so on this former city street, now closed to traffic, and turned left into the Carters' driveway.

Their home is an attractive brick structure, neatly landscaped, but in no way pretentious. I walked to the front entrance, rang the bell and stepped back.

President Carter opened the door. He flashed his famous grin and ushered me in. I was led to a sitting room at the right of the main entrance. We exchanged a few pleasantries, and then Rosalynn joined us. Immediately I came to the point of my visit.

"President Carter," I said, "I'm here as a neighbor, because you and Mrs. Carter have expressed interest in Habitat for Humanity."

I reviewed rapidly for them the ways in which they had been involved to date. I went on to say that what they had already done was deeply appreciated, but I wanted to find out if they had a greater interest than they had thus far expressed. Then I asked directly: "Are you simply *interested* in Habitat for Humanity, or are you *very interested?*"

President Carter smiled broadly, looked at Rosalynn and then quietly replied, "We're very interested."

"Well," I responded, "what do we do with that interest?"

He told me to go back to my office and think of ways in which they could be helpful. "Write me a letter," he said, "outlining the ideas you have on how we might be involved." He paused, then added, "And don't be bashful. List all of the ways you think we can help. After we get your letter, we'll think about the matter some more and decide precisely what we can and should do."

We talked for another twenty minutes or so about the work of Habitat. Then I left. My head was absolutely reeling with ideas on how a former president of the United States and his wife could be helpful to Habitat for Humanity.

Back in the office, I phoned David Rowe immediately. I asked him to begin listing ways in which President and Mrs. Carter might become involved. I also called several more Habitat directors and asked for their ideas. Then I convened the office staff and asked them to shift their thinking into high gear on this subject. I prayed and thought long and hard for days. I did not want to rush this letter. I wanted to make sure no good suggestion was left out. Sixteen days later, I finally mailed my letter to President and Mrs. Carter.

February 8, 1984

President and Mrs. Jimmy Carter
Plains, GA 31780

Dear President and Mrs. Carter,

First of all, I want to thank both of you profusely for meeting with me at your home, and for giving generously of your time to discuss Habitat for Humanity.

Your words of encouragement and affirmation meant a great deal to me personally, and to all of us who work closely with this growing venture. Your assurance of your strong interest in the work causes hope and rejoicing among us.

As you requested, I returned to the office and engaged everyone in prayer and discussion about how you could be most helpful to Habitat for Humanity. You asked us not to be bashful in suggesting possibilities. As you can see from the long list, we have taken you at your word!

1) *One of you could serve as a Director or an Advisor of Habitat for Humanity.* By separate mail I am sending you a full list of directors, advisors, and Habitat project representatives. We are authorized by our Articles of Incorporation to have twenty-five directors. We currently have twenty-two directors. New people are elected each year at the fall meeting.

Directors meet twice a year, in the spring and fall, always in a different Habitat project location. Advisors meet with the directors once a year, in the fall. Directors are *expected* to attend meetings. Advisors are *urged* to attend. Most directors pay their own way, and advisors travel at their own expense. Both advisors and directors are encouraged to help with administrative expenses of Habitat. Most give generously to those expenses.

2) *Make media contacts.* The Salvation Army, CARE, Red Cross, the Boy Scouts, and similar organizations have immediate name recognition. Habitat for Humanity does not. You went from Jimmy *Who?* to Jimmy Carter, a worldwide household name, in a short span of time. If you could make contacts with the appropriate media people to encourage them to do something on Habitat for Humanity, that would be *most* helpful.

3) *Put us in contact with key foundation and corporation people who could be helpful.* In 1983 we raised about $2,400,000 from all sources for all projects. This money came almost entirely from individuals and churches. Practically nothing was given by corporations and foundations. That ought to change. We also need equipment—trucks, construction tools, office computers, media equipment—that could either be donated or sold at a reduced price.

4) *Write a letter to your personal friends telling them about Habitat for Humanity and your support of it.*

5) *Write an endorsement letter in a direct mail campaign soliciting support for Habitat.*

6) *Put us in touch with other well-known persons who might want to be helpful to Habitat.*

7) *Do a public service announcement for Habitat for use on television and radio.*

8) *Do a thirty minute videotape interview with me about Habitat for Humanity.* It would then be made available throughout the country for church school classes and discussion groups.

9) *As Southern Baptists, you could be specifically helpful in encour-*

aging more support from them by writing letters to key people. As you know, Habitat for Humanity is totally ecumenical. We have a lot of Southern Baptist support, but not nearly in proportion to what other denominations are doing. We want to change that.

10) *Let us arrange speaking engagements in a few key areas of the United States.* You would attract large crowds, and of course we would actively promote the events, in accordance with appropriate guidelines set in consultation with you.

11) *Visit some overseas Habitat projects.* You would gain a more in depth understanding of the work of Habitat in the third world, and at the same time the trip would give Habitat international visibility and credibility.

12) *Visit U.S. Habitat projects.*

13) *Be a volunteer.* If you would work on the Americus construction crew for one day, it would set a great example. You, Rosalynn, could help either in the office or on the construction crew—we don't discriminate against women! We would document your volunteer work on film and let your example inspire others.

14) *Personally contribute money.* You have already done this, and your gifts are deeply appreciated. Your example of regular contributions will mean much more than the actual dollars you may give.

15) *Pray.* I am a strong believer in the power of prayer. Your regular prayers are as important as anything on this long list.

As I said above, this is a long list, and I know that you may be able to respond positively to only a few of the suggestions. On the other hand, this list may prompt you to think of other ways in which you could be helpful.

Again, I want to thank you for your friendship, encouragement, and support.

Respectfully,

Millard Fuller

A few days later, I received a call from Faye Dill. President Carter wanted to see me again at their home. I was filled with excitement as I traversed once more the nine miles between the Habitat office in Americus and the Carters' home in Plains.

President Carter again welcomed me at their front door and ushered me into the same sitting room.

"You wrote a good letter," he said. "Rosalynn and I have been talking about it, and we think we can help in most of the ways you suggest." He picked up my letter from a lamp stand beside his chair, reviewing the items individually and making brief comments about each one. "On fund raising," he said, "we're still raising money for the Presidential Library, so I'll have to focus my main efforts there for a while longer. But fairly soon I expect I can do more in this regard."

On the matter of his working on the Americus building crew, he simply said I should check with Faye Dill to find a clear date. He wanted to do that as soon as possible.

He would join the board of directors, and Rosalynn would be an advisor. Both of them wanted to serve actively in these capacities and attend meetings regularly.

I left their home elated. The Carters were obviously sincere in wanting to help Habitat for Humanity in significant ways. And I knew that their involvement would make a profound impact, the long term effects of which we could not even imagine.

A month later, Jimmy Carter came to volunteer a day's work on the construction crew in Americus. He arrived ten minutes early for morning devotions, then labored diligently all day. I already knew the president was a talented carpenter who had crafted beautiful furniture for his own home and for friends. But to have him working here beside our Habitat crew, putting up framing for Dorothy and Willie Solomon's new house on Habitat Street, was just fantastic.

The occasion was not without incident. At one point, when the crew was lifting a set of framing into place, it slipped and began to topple right toward President Carter. One of the Secret Service men quickly jumped between him and the falling wall, grabbing it just in time to prevent a possible serious injury. Later, there was a flurry of excitement when one of the workmen fired a little gun that shoots a concrete nail through the wood framing into the concrete floor. The loud *BANG!* of the gun again brought the Secret Service men to a sudden alert. Some nervous laughs followed as everyone realized what was going on.

At noon, we gathered for sandwiches and salad in "Peace" house.

(All of the fourteen houses which we have gradually renovated for office space and volunteer housing have received names like "Peace" and "Justice" and "Amigo.") Some of the work crew and several staff people joined us for a relaxed time of sharing and fellowship. During the meal, I talked with President Carter concerning the video interview I had mentioned in my letter. We both felt that it would be valuable to have a third person for such a production, and we discussed several possibilities. Then the name of Andrew Young was mentioned. Everyone promptly agreed that he would be perfect, if he would consent to do it. President Carter asked, "Where's a phone?"

"Next door."

"Good," President Carter responded. "I'll call him right now."

We went into "Agape" house, and President Carter phoned Mayor Young at his office in Atlanta. Because of our seven-hundred-mile walk which passed through Atlanta the previous year, and because of the budding Habitat project in his city, the mayor already knew about Habitat for Humanity. He was supportive, and he readily accepted our invitation to join in making an audio-visual program about the work of Habitat.

Wallace Braud, our media director, immediately began working on the logistical details. The filming, we decided, would take place in Mayor Young's back yard in Atlanta. A date was set for the following month, April of 1984.

President Carter and I met at the Young home on a beautiful spring day. With Mayor Young moderating, the three of us talked about the great need in our world for shelter for God's people, and about the imperative in the gospel for us to act to change things. We talked specifically about the growing work of Habitat for Humanity in Atlanta, Americus, throughout the United States, and around the world. The result was a twenty-five-minute video cassette program called, "World in Need . . . Opportunity to Share."

In subsequent months, hundreds of these cassettes were shipped all over the United States, and to Canada and Europe as well, for use by church and community groups and television stations. The program continues to be shown widely, and is an effective aid in telling the Habitat story.

After the filming, we were invited into the Youngs' home for refreshments and visiting. During the conversation, Mayor Young's wife, Jean, suggested that their daughter, Paula, might be interested in volunteering with Habitat. Paula had recently graduated from Duke University, and her mother said Paula had often expressed a desire to work for a time in Africa. I left my address and asked her to have Paula write me.

A few weeks later, I got a note from Paula saying she did indeed have an interest in working with Habitat. On July 8, 1984, Paula arrived in Americus for orientation, and six months later she flew to Uganda to work with the Habitat project in Gulu, and to teach in one of the local elementary schools.

Jimmy and Rosalynn Carter were not only helping us with fund-raising and publicity. Now they were indirectly responsible for bringing us another first rate volunteer for Africa.

And their involvement had barely gotten under way.

Poverty housing in Ntondo, Zaire *(left)*, Papua New Guinea *(below, left)*, and Americus, Georgia *(below, right)*.

Right: A sturdy new house built next to this family's former shack in Haiti.

Above: The 700-mile walk to Indianapolis begins with a crowd of escorts, including Rosalynn and Amy Carter.

Below: And . . . they're off! Heading north toward Atlanta.

Above: The walk was successful, but there was still some agony of "de feet."

Below: Tired but jubilant marchers cross a bridge in Louisville, Kentucky, on the last leg of their journey.

Jimmy Carter discusses plans for Lillie Mae Bowens's new house as they stand next to her old shack.

Left: Raising the frame of a new Habitat house in Americus.
Right: Jimmy and Rosalynn relax on Habitat's office steps.

7

Two Weeks at Hard Labor

n the spring of 1984, a few weeks after his work day in Americus, President Carter was in New York City for a speaking engagement. At our invitation, he went to see the Habitat project on East Sixth Street, where a six-story tenement was being gutted prior to renovation.

Rob DeRocker, director of the New York project, led President Carter carefully up five flights of a temporary wooden staircase which had been completed by volunteers just two days earlier. As they stood on the roof of the abandoned building and surveyed the urban wasteland below them, President Carter remarked, "I can see you've got some work ahead of you here, Rob. Let Millard know if there's anything I can do to help you. He's my boss."

Rob replied quickly, "Why don't you come back with a group from your church for a work week?"

"We'll think about it," was the reply.

When Rob called me to report on President Carter's visit, I

was amazed and encouraged by his response to Rob's suggestion. What a terrific idea! I got in touch with the president when he returned to Plains. Was he really interested in leading a work group to New York City? The answer was prompt and affirmative. Well, if President Carter had designated me as his "boss," I certainly wouldn't hesitate to order him to get busy on this great idea!

We began immediately to make plans for this extraordinary work party. Ted Swisher, who coordinates all U.S. Habitat projects, and I met with President Carter at his home, and we settled on the first week in September. We would charter a bus and leave Americus at noon on Saturday, September 1, riding all night in order to arrive in New York by Sunday afternoon. Work would begin on Monday morning and continue until Friday afternoon of that week. The work group would consist not only of people from the Maranatha Baptist Church in Plains, but also of volunteers from other parts of Georgia, and even a few from other states.

We could charter a Trailways bus for a little under $4000. Everyone would pay $125 plus another $25 for food, and all expenses of the trip would be covered. Linda and Deen Day Smith, from Atlanta, would be in charge of food buying, and with several other work campers they would prepare meals in the kitchen of Metro Baptist Church in New York, where we would be staying. Noon meals would be carted over to Emmanuel Presbyterian Church, across East Sixth Street from the building being renovated, to be served in their fellowship hall.

Anticipation kept growing, both in New York and in Georgia, as September 1 approached. Phones in the Habitat office in Americus rang constantly as reporters from newspapers and radio and television stations around the country inquired about our plans.

"Is President Carter really going to ride on the bus all the way to New York?"

"Is it true that he intends to sleep in a bunk bed at the Metro Baptist Church?"

"Is he actually planning to do *physical work* on the building?"

The press reaction ranged from skeptical to astonished to genuinely impressed.

On the morning of our departure, the front of the Habitat office building displayed big banners welcoming the work campers and wishing us all *bon voyage*. Nearly a hundred people came to see us off, and during a brief farewell ceremony Linda presented the president with a pair of bib overalls on which she had appliquéd the Habitat logo. She also gave both Carters Habitat T-shirts.

Following a farewell luncheon in our Visitors' Center, eighteen people boarded the bus, and amid cheers of "Habitat Oyée!" we headed north toward Atlanta. (Rosalynn Carter was unable to travel on the bus because of a previous commitment. She flew to New York and joined us on Monday.)

Two and a half hours later we pulled into the parking lot of the First Baptist Church in College Park, a suburb of Atlanta, to pick up eighteen more people. Among them were the pastor of that church, Dr. J. W. Wallis, and President Carter's efficient scheduling secretary, Nancy Konigsmark. Most of the other people were from Atlanta, Ellijay, and Calhoun, but one person, Esther Fein of the *New York Times*, had flown down to ride back north with us, and her experiences resulted in a front page story on Labor Day. Ron Taylor of the *Atlanta Constitution* joined us, and so did Jim Newton, another reporter, and Paul Obregon, a photographer. Jim and Paul worked with us all week, and later collaborated on a fourteen-page article about Habitat which appeared in the Southern Baptist magazine, *Missions USA*.

We were now thirty-six strong. Filled with expectation, we headed north, and as night was descending we arrived in Columbia, South Carolina. A new Habitat project forming in that city had asked us to stop there and have supper with them. We pulled up in front of Ladson Presbyterian Church, the oldest black congregation in Columbia. The sidewalk was full of media people anxious to get an interview with President Carter.

After several minutes of visiting and shaking hands, we were escorted into the church. A superb meal had been prepared for us by the local folks—fried chicken, green beans, rice and mushrooms, iced tea, blueberry pie, pecan pie, and little lemon cakes. What a sendoff!

Following the dinner, there was a brief time of greetings and expressions of appreciation on all sides. When I introduced President Carter, he spoke with great feeling about his growing involvement with Habitat. He stated that the Habitat board was the only one he served on out of the dozens of invitations he had received since he had left the White House, and that he was making a lifetime commitment to the ministry of Habitat for Humanity. He concluded, "Habitat for Humanity can make a profound impact on Christendom. I am proud to be a part of it."

We pulled out of Columbia about 9:00 P.M. Saturday, full of good food and good feelings and ready for the long ride to New York. But by the time we stopped at the Trailways terminal in Washington, D.C., for breakfast early Sunday morning, I was having less comfortable feelings. My six-foot-four frame was not designed for sleeping on bus seats.

About 10:30 A.M. we turned off the New Jersey Turnpike at the little town of Bellmawr to attend worship. The Secret Service had gone ahead to find a church and to notify the pastor we would be there. When the bus stopped in the parking lot of a small Conservative Baptist Church, I got off with President Carter. The pastor emerged as we approached. He was obviously awed by the presence of a former president. Extending his hand to Jimmy Carter, he exclaimed nervously, "There will be two important persons in church this morning: you and God!" I didn't ask whether he meant in that order.

Following the service, we continued on the last leg of our long journey. Just outside the Lincoln Tunnel leading into Manhattan, we picked up a two-car police escort. They led us through the tunnel to the Metro Baptist Church, which is on Fortieth Street, near the Port Authority Bus Terminal. It was mid-afternoon, Sunday, September 2. We had finally arrived.

A welcoming throng crowded in front of the church, including many Habitat folks and dozens of media people. A large sign draped across the church entrance read:

WELCOME TO NEW YORK CITY
PRESIDENT AND ROSALYNN CARTER AND THE
HABITAT WORK TEAM
FROM THE METRO BAPTIST FAMILY

We quickly unloaded our baggage. Bunk beds for women were on the third floor and for men on the fourth. Then we reboarded the bus to visit the building where we would be working, at 742 East Sixth Street on Manhattan's Lower East Side. Television crews from all the major networks would be there early Monday morning to film the project and to interview Jimmy Carter. We needed to get organized so that work would be under way when the "Good Morning, America" cameras arrived.

Weeks of advance preparation for the work team had already been done by New York Habitat people and by Ted Swisher. Ted had gone up from Americus a week earlier to purchase materials, round up tools, and plan work schedules. We learned that during our stay we would be prying up rotten flooring, shoveling half a century's accumulation of dirt and debris off of the first floor, replacing rotten beams, putting down new sub-flooring, and completely replacing the old roof.

In addition to the thirty-six people who rode up on the bus, our small Habitat army was reinforced by some additional recruits. A dozen other volunteers flew or drove in from Pennsylvania, Maryland, Colorado, New Jersey, Massachusetts, and upstate New York to join us for the week.

On Monday morning, we divided into small groups and began our various assigned tasks on six precarious floors. Media people were scrambling all over the place. It wasn't long before Linda ripped up some old boards on the first floor and discovered a pile of bones.

"Quick, get Schley Gatewood!" she called. "What if these are human bones?"

Schley, a medical doctor from Americus, climbed down from some floor above Linda and spent a few minutes examining the collection of old bones and bone fragments. Then, to everyone's relief, he announced they were *not* human bones. Our first crisis had been averted.

A press conference had been scheduled at 10:30 A.M., and scores of reporters and photographers gathered behind police barricades on Sixth Street in front of the building. I went down with Rob DeRocker and Jimmy Carter to greet them.

The president spoke briefly about his interest and involvement in Habitat. He explained specifically what we planned to do with this building, and then invited questions. With a presidential election just two months away, reporters wanted to ask about politics, but Jimmy Carter sidestepped these queries, emphasizing Habitat instead.

At one point a reporter inquired, "Isn't this kind of project exactly what President Reagan is talking about in terms of self-help, with private citizens doing things to build up the country and help those in need?"

"Yes, I think it is, but talking about doing is one thing. Doing is something else!"

"Isn't it unusual for a former vice-president to be involved in something like this?"

"Not having been a vice-president, I don't feel I can answer that question."

There were great peals of laughter, and then the president added, "That question, I suppose, only goes to show how fleeting fame is!"

More laughter. And no more questions from that reporter.

"Will you work all week?"

"Yes."

"Will Mrs. Carter also be working this week?"

"Yes. She'll arrive later today to work with us for the remainder of the time."

"Are you really sleeping in a bunk bed at Metro Baptist Church?"

"Yes. In a top bunk."

"What made you sacrifice a week to come here instead of going to the Virgin Islands?"

"It's not a sacrifice. I've worked hard all my life, and carpentry is nothing new for me. I'm enjoying it. It's great to meet new friends and do something to help others at the same time."

That summed it up. I think the skeptical journalists gave up looking for political quotes and began to enjoy talking to Habitat's illustrious volunteer.

At the conclusion of the news conference, David Hartman, host of "Good Morning, America," walked up. He had interviewed

President Carter earlier in the morning by remote hook-up from the ABC midtown studio. President Carter had invited him, as well as every other interviewer, to come down to visit and work with us. We gave him a tour of the first couple of floors. President Carter resumed his work on the second floor, and I took Mr. Hartman through the remaining four floors to the roof. We couldn't talk him into taking up a hammer and helping, but NBC's John Palmer, who interviewed President Carter on "The Today Show" that Monday morning, did accept the invitation. He stayed for several hours and worked up quite a sweat.

As the volunteers labored steadily throughout the building, crowds gathered on the street below. Periodically they began chanting, "Jimmy, Jimmy, Jimmy!" Whenever the president appeared at the second story window, a great cheer went up. Spectators continued to come every day, and each time they saw President Carter or Rosalynn, they cheered. When the Carters emerged from the building for lunch or at the end of the day, there was always a large group waiting for a chance to get a handshake or an autograph.

Phone calls began to come in to the New York Habitat office so rapidly that we had to send a couple of our work team members there to help. Many callers were simply curious about what the Carters were doing, but some people wanted to know how they could help with the project. Donations of money were offered along with pledges of free labor, building materials, and other supplies and services.

On Wednesday, Paschall McGuinnes, President of the New York District Council of the United Brotherhood of Carpenters and Joiners of America, came to the building to present a check for five hundred dollars and a gold union card to President Carter. He also pledged sheetrock and other materials, plus the assistance of several apprentice carpenters. Four young men from the union helped for the remainder of the week. Mr. McGuinnes also presented everyone in our work group with union caps and nail aprons.

The Sub-Contractors Trade Association phoned to pledge a gift of two thousand dollars. The Hittner Truck Rental Company offered to furnish, rent-free, any of their trucks for the duration of the work on the building. A man from New Jersey, who heard about the project on his car radio, drove to the site to provide a large box of nails and a collection of tools. And a lady from the Bronx took a subway all the way to the Lower East Side to present a flowering plant to the president. It was placed on the fire escape in front of the building, symbolizing the new hope that had blossomed in that blighted neighborhood.

One of the most meaningful calls came from an elderly man on Long Island who had lived in the then-elegant building seventy-eight years earlier. He was thrilled to know that this dilapidated tenement would be revived, and he offered a donation of a thousand dollars.

An exciting and completely unexpected gift was received on Tuesday evening. We had decided ahead of time that we would eat at a nice restaurant one evening while we were in New York. So we all cleaned up following a long work day, piled on the bus, and headed for the Silver Palace Restaurant in Chinatown.

We were served a magnificent six-course meal: fried shrimp stuffed with pork, delicate beef strips, corn soup, an exotic chicken recipe, an unusual rice dish, fish in a lemon sauce. For dessert we had honeydew melon, canteloupe and other fruits, and fortune cookies. The food was wonderful, and so was the fellowship. Sometimes the kidding and clowning were so hilarious it was hard to eat.

At the conclusion of the meal, everyone paid seventeen dollars. Suddenly, the manager held the wad of money high and announced he was giving it all back to Habitat to help renovate the building! A huge cheer went up. "Silver Palace Oyée!"

For five days, work at the building went on at a fever pitch. Old plaster was knocked down, rotten and charred beams were ripped out and replaced. Debris was tossed out the windows at such a steady pace that there was a perpetual cloud of dust rising from the back of the building. Many work campers had to wear protective masks. By week's end, the pile of splintered boards, broken beams, crumbling plaster, and other trash was two stories high!

Each workday began with short devotions at the Metro Church during breakfast. Then the bus that had brought us from Georgia delivered us to the job site by 8:00 A.M. Our usual workday ended at five in the evening, with an hour-long break for lunch. But we departed from the usual as much as we followed it. Often we would arrive before eight, take only a thirty-minute lunch break, and work until 5:30 or 6:00 P.M. One work camper who never wanted to quit at the end of the day was Jimmy Carter. And on a couple of mornings he jogged to the site from the church, a distance of about three miles, and was on the job an hour ahead of everyone else.

Climbing around and working in this gutted shell of a building was hazardous. While the new roof was being constructed, we could look straight down through six stories to the ground in many places. With so many amateur builders among our volunteers, it was remarkable that we had only one real injury during the week. Rev. James Holt, pastor of the First Baptist Church of Ellijay, Georgia, was helping to take some boards up the stairs, and his foot slipped through a hole on one of the temporary steps. The flesh was torn away from the shin bone on his right leg. Fortunately, no bones were broken and no arteries were cut, but forty stitches were required to close the wound, and he was forced to return home.

(James Holt was not only undaunted by his painful experience— he was positively inspired. His leg healed rapidly, and he and others plunged in to launch a Habitat project in their home area. In October of 1985, they were officially accepted for affiliation as North Central Georgia Habitat for Humanity.)

On Wednesday evening, all of us participated in the regular midweek prayer service at Metro Baptist Church. Of course the service was not exactly "regular" with a former president there in addition to about a hundred other visitors, including our work campers. We presented a plaque to the church commemorating the week, and Rev. Gene Bolin, on behalf of the church, presented each member of the work team with a neatly sawed piece of old beam from the building bearing a plaque on the front reading, "In appreciation for volunteer work providing housing for the poor." A new hammer rested on brackets above the plaque.

The grand finale of the week came on Friday evening. A tremendous crowd filled St. Bartholomew's Episcopal Church at 50th Street and Park Avenue for the special Habitat celebration we call a "Habitation."

At the end of an exciting evening of stirring music, resounding speeches, and praising the Lord together, hard hats were passed down the pews for the offering. The money was then dumped into wheelbarrows and pushed up the aisles to the front of the sanctuary. That night over ten thousand dollars was given. Some twenty thousand more in money and materials had come in during the week.

As we prepared for the return trip on Saturday, we knew our presence had made a difference in the New York City project. In addition, millions more people throughout the nation had now at least heard about the work of Habitat for Humanity. The week had been a success, and there was rejoicing, laughter, and singing as the weary work campers began their long ride home.

But by the time the bus pulled into Atlanta at 4:30 on Sunday morning, there hadn't been a sound from anyone for a long time.

After the New York work camp, it became clear that Jimmy and Rosalynn Carter had indeed signed on as longterm Habitat volunteers. It wasn't hard to find lots more jobs for them to do.

In the fall of 1984, they went on a personal trip to several South American countries, and made their last stop the Habitat project in Puno, Peru. Thanks to media coverage of their stay, as well as meetings with Peruvian leaders where the Carters discussed the purpose of their visit, the whole country had heard about Habitat by the time they left.

On October 11, 1984, the Carters flew directly from Peru to Amarillo, Texas, for their first Habitat board meeting. President Carter attended all of the board sessions, participating in consultations without ever seeking to dominate them. Fellow board members appreciated how quickly he became one of the group, contributing positively whenever he was familiar with the matter under discussion and listening intently when he was not.

Rosalynn was equally involved, attending meetings with the advisors and United States project representatives. One afternoon she led a two-hour workshop on ways to tell the Habitat story, sharing strategies for getting media coverage which she had learned during political campaigns. Following the Amarillo meetings, Mrs. Carter promoted Habitat in television appearances and newspaper interviews. And she made a major contribution to several projects around the country by hosting fundraisers and dedicating houses.

A few weeks later, President Carter and I traveled together to New York City to speak at a luncheon hosted by the Chemical Bank, kicking off a campaign to raise ten million dollars for Habitat's tenth anniversary in 1986. More than one hundred leaders of corporations, foundations, and church agencies from the New York area attended. As a result of that luncheon and follow-up contacts which we made, over a hundred thousand dollars was pledged, and our campaign was on its way.

To provide ideas and direction for the ten-million-dollar campaign, we needed a special planning committee. Once again I approached Jimmy Carter, and he agreed to serve as chairman. By the time of our first meeting at his Atlanta office on February 21, 1985, we had assembled a dynamite committee: George Anderson of Thornhill, Ontario, Canada; Landrum Bolling of Washington, D.C.; Ted Engstrom of Monrovia, California; Louis Fischer of Jupiter, Florida; Keith Jaspers of Springfield, Missouri; Robert E. Johnson of Chicago, Illinois; John Pritchard of Liberty, Missouri; David Rowe of Melrose, Massachusetts; Deen Day Smith of Atlanta, Georgia; Ron Yates of Acton, Massachusetts; and Andrew Young of Atlanta, Georgia. (Five members were later added to this committee: Neil Anderson of Amulree, Ontario, Canada; Keith Paul of Nashville, Tennessee; Ted and Vada Stanley of Westport, Connecticut; and Glegg Watson of Stamford, Connecticut.)

Fundraising ideas for individuals and churches came thick and fast at this meeting, and everyone in the group was committed to work in personal ways as well. But the most creative fundraiser of all was undoubtedly Jimmy Carter.

For example, shortly after the Atlanta meeting, he learned that a sporting goods company had run his photograph in one of their ads without consulting him. He asked his attorney to phone the head office and inquire pointedly who gave them permission to use his picture in an ad campaign.

"Uh-oh," was the reply. "What do we do now?"

"The president has instructed me to tell you that he is not asking for anything personally. But he thought it would be nice for you to send a contribution of ten thousand dollars to Habitat for Humanity."

Within a few days we received the check.

A few months later, the Purina Company contacted the Carters requesting permission to feature their cat, Misty Malarky, in the company's 1986 calendar. Once again the picture was approved—on condition that a gift of five thousand dollars be made to Habitat.

Invitations to speak to colleges, conventions, and every kind of organization poured into Jimmy Carter's office daily. He could say yes to very few. But often when he did, he accepted on condition that Habitat for Humanity receive a generous donation.

Having the president on our side was invaluable in many ways that had nothing to do with fundraising. In 1984 volunteers Roger and Barbara Sneller of Zeeland, Michigan, had completed their orientation and were waiting for visas to India, where they would work in a new Habitat project in Khammam. For no apparent reason, their applications were rejected. The Snellers went through all the paperwork a second time, and they were rejected again. At this point I contacted President Carter, who promptly sent a handwritten letter to Prime Minister Indira Gandhi, asking for her intervention. Within a few days we got the visas.

In January 1985, the Habitat dump truck was suddenly confiscated in Gulu, Uganda, by the Ugandan Army. All our efforts to get it back were fruitless. After a month without transportation at that project, I again requested President Carter's help. Another handwritten letter was dispatched, this time to President Milton Obote. We got the truck back promptly—personally delivered by General Basilio Okello, who overthrew President Obote six months later!

Throughout the spring of 1985, President Carter kept in touch with the progress on the New York project. The mammoth job of renovating that gutted tenement was moving slowly, dependent largely upon weekend volunteer groups. Habitat's fall 1985 board meeting would be hosted by the New York City affiliate, and the dedication of their first building was to be the grand finale of that gathering. To give the project another shot in the arm, President Carter offered to go back during the summer of 1985 for a second work week. And on July 29 we did just that.

As we planned this second effort, we found that many of our 1984 work campers were able to sign on again, and other Habitat friends joined us to fill the remaining spaces. Once again we rode the bus all night Saturday (after stopping in Charlotte, North Carolina, to speak at a huge meeting sponsored by the Charlotte Habitat project), breakfasted in the Washington Trailways station, and headed on for New York City.

At 10:30 A.M. on Sunday, July 30, we pulled off the New Jersey Turnpike to look for a place to worship. But this time Jimmy Carter had not sent the Secret Service ahead scouting. He decided he just wanted to pop in on some church. So we drove into Edison, New Jersey, a few miles south of New York City. We had difficulty locating a service, because we discovered that in the summer churches in that part of the country often worship earlier than usual. Every one we stopped at was either in the middle of their service or had already concluded it.

Finally we asked at a fire station for a church with an eleven o'clock service. They directed us up a dead-end street a couple of blocks away to a small Lutheran church. When the bus parked in front of the building, we saw a sign: *St. Stephen's Evangelical Lutheran Church—Sunday Service, 10:30 A.M.* It was about five minutes before eleven.

"What do you want to do?" President Carter asked.

"We don't have time to go anywhere else," I responded. "Let's go in. We're in time for the sermon!"

"Okay, let's go!"

Everyone piled out, and thirty-three of us marched up to the front door of the sanctuary. There was no way we were going to be able to avoid creating a commotion during the worship service, no matter how silently we tried to enter. When we pulled open the big door, however, we were astonished. Not a soul was inside!

Just then we noticed a couple of children outside an adjacent building, so we went over. As we approached, a lady opened the door. We learned that the whole congregation was inside, having an eighty-fifth birthday party for a member who had been brought from a nursing home. As we walked in, the people recognized President Carter. They began to stand and clap.

St. Stephen's had held their service at 9:30 A.M. The posted time for worship announced their fall schedule, and like the rest of the churches in the area, this congregation held summer services an hour earlier.

The pastor, E. Walter Cleckley, Jr., a young man whose home town turned out to be Augusta, Georgia, came over to greet us. He was absolutely astounded that President Carter had come to his church. (Later a comment from the pastor was quoted by a reporter: "When we give a party, we really give a *party!*") We apologized for barging in on the congregation, and asked if we could simply use their sanctuary for worship. We told the pastor we had several preachers with us, including a seminary president, and we could put together our own service.

"Of course you may use the sanctuary," he replied. "But if you'd like us to, we'll be glad to repeat our service for you."

After a couple of minutes of discussion, it was decided. They would do their service again. The organist was still there, and the pastor still had his sermon notes. We returned to the sanctuary, and most of the church members came with us.

The sermon could not have been more timely. It was based on Scripture from the second chapter of Ephesians. In the concluding verses of that chapter, Paul says,

> You are not foreigners or strangers any longer; you are now fellow-citizens with God's people and members of the family of God. You, too, are built upon the foundation laid by the apostles and prophets, being the corner stone, Christ Jesus himself. He is the one who holds the whole building together and makes it grow into a sacred temple dedicated to the Lord. In union with him you too are also

being built together with all the others into a place where God lives through his Spirit (vv. 19–22).

Cornerstones . . . foundations . . . buildings! And none of us there were strangers; we were fellow citizens with all of God's people!

We listened in awe. As the excited young pastor preached about building on a solid foundation a dwelling place for members of the family of God, I doubt whether he had ever had a congregation who gave him more rapt attention.

At the close of the service, there were warm thank-yous all around, and we went on to New York rejoicing. The Lord had prepared a sermon especially for us.

Returning to the gradually emerging apartment building on East Sixth Street, we shared another week of hard labor and rich fellowship. This time, most of the families who would live in the nineteen apartments had been chosen, and the homesteaders enriched our fellowship still more as they worked beside us all week.

And this time our fundraising for the project was increased by a great idea. Ellen Baer, a New York Habitat board member, had contacted area churches, asking members to sponsor President Carter's week of work at so much an hour. Many people responded, intrigued with this opportunity to hire the president as their carpenter. On Friday evening, Richard and Peg Alpin of Long Island, who had pledged twenty-five dollars an hour, came to see what was going on. When they learned that President Carter had put in fifty-one hours of work during the week, Rich responded immediately, "Hey, now I have to pay time and a half!"

Someone did some quick figuring, and came up with the total $1,412.50. "Make it an even fifteen hundred!" said Rich.

He was beaming, and so were we. He left us with a check for that amount, and promised to continue his support by returning to the building with work groups from his church.

Thanks to the presence of the Carters, our second Lower East Side work camp drew still more national media attention for Habitat, and more visitors from New York area businesses, churches, and foundations. And shortly after this effort ended, the president began making plans to visit the Habitat project in Nicaragua in February 1986, and in July of that year to lead another work group, this time at the Chicago Habitat project.

There is no way to measure the vast amounts of money, materials, and good will which have been generated for Habitat by the energies of our two most famous volunteers. But we are inexpressibly grateful.

Jimmy and Rosalynn Carter Oyée!

8

On the Shoulders
of Volunteers

Habitat always moves on the shoulders of volunteers. Jimmy and Rosalynn Carter have joined a host of these energetic partners of all ages who serve around the world with whatever skills they possess. And their number keeps growing.

One of the characteristics of Habitat's ministry which often produces comments of amazement is the remarkable cross-section of people who are working together. We invite anyone who is interested to share in this effort. Opportunities to help are unlimited, whether it's in a volunteer's own hometown or on the other side of the globe—or anywhere in between.

When the word "volunteer" is first mentioned, particularly in connection with work projects, many people think of high school and college students. And Habitat programs everywhere have indeed benefited enormously from the labors of thousands of youth who donate a week or a month of their vacations to work at a project site and provide a solid boost to local construction efforts.

Howard Taylor, pastor of First Baptist Church in Woodstown, New Jersey, and a board member of Salem County Habitat, has led two summer work groups from his congregation to the Habitat project on Johns Island, South Carolina. Howard stated that there are few experiences in the church which leave a more lasting impression on the people involved.

"If it is carefully planned," Howard said, "the trip produces an important sense of accomplishing something, even for unskilled people, in a short period of time. There is the valuable experience of working together to build, in a spirit of Christian fellowship. Lasting friendships are formed, and intergenerational understanding increases amazingly. It is fun to see adults astounded by the serious work teenagers can accomplish, and teenagers are equally surprised as they begin to view adults as people instead of authority figures.

"Each time we have taken a work group," Howard continued, "they have acquired a fresh sensitivity to the needs of others. And this is not limited just to people on the trip. The whole church feels a new connectedness to missions. Through fundraising, prayer vigils, farewell breakfasts at dawn, and welcome-home receptions afterward, the entire congregation gets involved, and people are still talking about these trips years later. The work camp experience is valuable far beyond whatever it costs to go."

Individual young people often decide to give a longer period of service before entering careers or graduate school. We have welcomed scores of talented volunteers in this category, and projects are eager to receive them.

Dan Roman of Mesa, Arizona, was one of these. In 1981 we received a glowing letter from Mobanda Mopenge in Ntondo, Zaire, about the work of Habitat in his village. Especially Mobanda thanked us for sending Dan, then twenty-two.

> Dan has arrived at his home! He doesn't need anything, because he is here with his brothers and sisters in Christ. And we have asked that he stay here until he gets grey hair on his head! We have given him the name of *Elombe:* Worker among Workers, Believer among Believers, Mighty Mover of the Work. The joy of Christ, and the love of God, I send to you because you chose to send him to us.

Jeremiah Wamachio, president of the Nzoia, Kenya Habitat project, wrote me a similar letter about volunteer Paul Haddad, of Belle River, Ontario, Canada. Said Jeremiah, "My boy, Paul, is God's gift to us!" Paul, who was sponsored by the Christian Service Corps, succeeded not only in building sturdy homes, but also in developing joy-filled relationships.

It is important to remember, however, that this joy in serving others is available at any age. And some of the most valuable people Habitat has been privileged to enlist as volunteers are retirees. These folks are exciting to know. At a stage in life when others seem inclined to settle permanently into their rocking chairs, senior citizens who volunteer with Habitat bring an energy and enthusiasm for the Lord's work which overcomes all sorts of obstacles, and seems to keep them young in the process.

One of these dynamic folks was Ellen Studley. A retired United Methodist minister and a missionary teacher in China from 1924 to 1951, she was living in Claremont, California, when she learned about Habitat for Humanity in 1981. Soon she was on a bus traveling for three days across the country. She arrived in Americus in mid-November of that year and served for six months. She was eighty-two at the time.

A Phi Beta Kappa from DePauw University, with a masters from Boston University and a B.D. from Union Theological Seminary, Ellen was a prolific writer. That skill was immediately put to use in Americus. She interviewed new volunteers daily, preparing creative press releases about them for their hometown newspapers. She also wrote scores of letters to friends and associates throughout the world, helping to spread the word about Habitat for Humanity and enlisting new supporters.

Often Ellen would lead us in morning devotions. She had a lot to share. One day she told of her experiences in China at the outbreak of World War II, and everyone in the Habitat office was sitting on the edge of their chairs. She survived internment at Weihsien. In her memoirs of those fateful months, Ellen wrote, "It is the things of the spirit which increase the survival chances. . . . Survival lies in the hope and faith and charity that grow as we shelter one another from depression of spirit, by evidences of selfless consideration and cheer."

Ellen has demonstrated that selfless consideration all her life. At age sixty-seven, she was told by doctors that she must never again "attempt anything strenuous physically or mentally." After that, she pastored two more churches in Indiana. She also tutored international students, and in 1984 she returned to China to visit old friends. Furthermore, following her first six months of service in Americus, she returned twice for shorter periods. There is absolutely *no* retirement age for Habitat volunteers!

Often volunteers come to us as families. Across the country from Ellen Studley lived the DuPont family of Laconia, New Hampshire. Paul and Kathie first came to Americus in August of 1981 with their children, Lisa and Jennifer, and their niece, Mary. They stayed for nine months, with Paul serving as building crew foreman and Kathie working in the office as typist, letter stuffer, and newsletter collator. Kathie found other ways to be helpful as well, including working as a liaison with local families who were receiving Habitat houses. The DuPonts were fully supported by their Congregational church in Laconia.

After their time in Americus, Paul and Kathie returned to their home town and helped to found the new Laconia, New Hampshire, Habitat affiliate. Soon that project spawned other projects in Warner and Plymouth.

In 1985, the DuPonts returned to Americus to volunteer for six months. This time a small son, Kevin, was also with them. Paul signed on again as building crew foreman. And Kathie, with a wealth of experience now from both Americus and New Hampshire, became an assistant to Ted Swisher in helping to coordinate the new projects that were mushrooming all over the place.

Some Habitat volunteers, in the middle years of life, are simply exploring a different direction. In 1982, at the age of forty, R. Dean DeBoer, a builder and a seminary graduate from Chapel Hill, North Carolina, went to Zaire to work on a new Habitat project in the village of Ikoko Bonginda. It soon became clear to Dean that this was the right direction for him. In his first letter home he wrote, "I've finally found my kind of town!" And every letter we received thereafter was signed, "Laughing in Zaire, R. Dean."

Returning to the United States three years later, Dean continued to volunteer time with Habitat—a project in Chapel Hill had been launched while he was overseas. Dean told us he considered his whole African experience an illustration of Jesus' promise: Seek the kingdom of God first, and then all the other things will be yours as well. He explained it this way:

> When I put aside what I had in the United States and took no thought for what might confront me in a strange land, simply offering myself, the rewards were marvelous. I didn't know it at the time, but when I landed in Kinshasa, Zaire, I was immediately a rich man. My volunteer stipend of $300 a month made me about the richest man in Ikoko Bonginda. I had plenty to eat, no worry about clothes, and I not only had a house larger than the one I had in North Carolina, but the village people also gave me a "son" to live with me, who honored me as a father. They gave me the use of a large boat and a "chauffeur" to drive it. They treated me as an honored guest in their village, and made me a chief among them. All of these things were indeed given to me. I marvel at the mercy and riches of God's love. If there is one thing I would wish to communicate to people, it is the joy of serving God's people in need, the riches and spiritual strength which can be found by those who truly seek first God's kingdom and His righteousness.

After his time in Africa, Dean returned to his home in North Carolina to find the Lord still fulfilling his needs.

> I made up a shopping list of things for the house, like sheets, pillow case, and kitchen items. I wondered what had become of the toaster oven I had left behind, but couldn't find. The very next day I walked into my house and on the table someone had left a bag. Inside I found two sheets, a pillow case, a towel, a loaf of banana bread, and a toaster oven! Seek first the kingdom of God, and all this other stuff *you can have!*

Many of Habitat's dedicated staff people are former volunteers who came and stayed. Ken Sauder, of Mount Joy, Pennsylvania, began working with Linda and me in Mbandaka, Zaire, in 1974. He went on to launch the project in Ntondo, Zaire, two years later. When he returned to the States he finished college and earned a masters degree in city planning from the University of Pennsylvania. But Ken felt the vision of Habitat for Humanity pulling him back, and in 1984 he came to Americus to become director of our work in Central and South America and the Caribbean.

In 1977 a young school teacher named Clive Rainey began volunteering his time in Americus. He went on to work in Kinshasa, Zaire; Gulu, Uganda; Gitega, Burundi, and Lilongwe, Malawi; and to become director of all African Habitat projects. Clive was particularly pleased about the Burundi program, which was under the direction of Bishop Ndorcimpa of the United Methodist Church. This project expected to be building entirely with Burundi volunteers by the end of 1986.

Bob and Kathy Geyer and their sons, Scott and Matthew, of Buffalo, New York, came to Americus as volunteers in 1982. Kathy worked in the mail room, typed, and assisted in the accounting department. Bob directed the home-building crew, and he also helped design and construct Habitat's office facilities. In 1985 Bob, who held a degree in accounting, laid down his hammer and blueprints and joined our staff as Director of Financial Services.

Wallace Braud learned about Habitat in 1982 when, as a staff person with the Episcopal Radio Television Foundation in Atlanta, he produced a program about this work. Shortly thereafter, he was in my office.

"I want to work with Habitat!"

"We need you, brother," I told him, "but we don't have the money to pay you. Habitat should have a media department to produce brochures and slide shows and movies and other promotional stuff. But right now, we just can't hire anybody."

Wallace's reply was quick and firm. "I'll work for free. My wife Nancy and I just have to have enough to live on."

Within a few weeks, Nancy, who was equally enthusiastic about the Habitat ministry, had found employment in Americus, and Wallace had become our media director. He served in that capacity as a volunteer for two years before he went on salary. When Wallace started getting paid, Nancy quit her job and became a Habitat volunteer, first as my assistant and later as editor of our newspaper, *Habitat World*.

On February 1, 1985, little Hannah Braud arrived and promptly became Habitat's youngest volunteer, serving as a model and good-will ambassador. We hope to add her to our staff soon after the turn of the century.

Of course, by far the largest group of volunteers in the Habitat family is made up of folks who serve at home. These people contribute, fundraise, and share their vision for decent housing wherever they happen to be. And every one of them is absolutely indispensable.

Frank Townsend of Lake Odessa, Michigan, is a retired carpenter. For years he has been crafting beautiful handmade furniture in a converted shed he calls his "Habitat workshop," and he has personally raised thousands of dollars in this way to build homes for God's needy children. Frank and Wilma Townsend and their family have been involved with a variety of other Habitat fundraising efforts, and they have also enlisted the assistance of the entire congregation of their church.

Every year the Hope Church of the Brethren, near Freeport, Michigan, holds a Fall Festival, of which Frank serves as chairman—and all the proceeds go to Habitat. In addition to displays of home-grown foods and handmade items, the celebration offers such delicacies as gallons of apple butter stirred in steaming outdoor kettles, sausage stuffed and smoked on the church grounds, and giant crocks of sauerkraut. Hope Church has raised enough money to build at least one house overseas every year since 1979!

When the project in Grand Rapids, Michigan, was getting under way in 1982, Frank was there, too, lending assistance and enthusiasm. We need thousands more serve-at-home volunteers like the Townsends!

Becky Cope is the founder and director, with her husband, Jerry, of a square dance resort on Belly's Creek Road in the little north Georgia town of Dillard. Gathering information from all over the United States, Becky published a book entitled *Square Dancers' Favorite Recipes and Stories.* Fifty cents from each copy sold would be donated to Habitat building programs in India and the Mississippi delta. Becky, an enthusiastic Christian, also encouraged square dance clubs to contribute on their own. She wrote me: "I am so excited about the possibilities of this project, not only for Habitat but for the *changed lives* that result from getting involved!"

In 1981 Rhodes and Lois Thompson moved to Enid, Oklahoma, where Rhodes became Assistant Professor of Preaching and Practical Theology at Phillips University Graduate Seminary. The Thompsons were already Habitat supporters, having inspired the congregation of the church Rhodes had just pastored (Memorial Boulevard Christian Church in St. Louis, Missouri) to build one house in Guatemala and another in Uganda. Now Rhodes and Lois, who had also served four years as missionaries in Japan, became owners of a modest home for the first time in their lives. They decided to launch a personal campaign to provide decent housing for others.

Rhodes often received requests for speaking engagements at churches and retreats. He and Lois began to dedicate these occasions to third world Christian ministries, and to channel all his honoraria to these ventures. By 1986 the portion sent to Habitat had built *twelve* houses: two in Guatemala, four in Haiti, one in Peru, one in India, and four in Nicaragua. He and Lois had also bought and given away more than three hundred copies of *Love in the Mortar Joints*. And I was not surprised to learn in late spring of 1985 that a new Habitat affiliate was organizing in the city of Enid, Oklahoma.

Meanwhile, the Thompsons' daughter, Jody, decided to teach an aerobics course in Enid and send her fees to Habitat, providing enough to pay half the cost of a house in Guatemala. Another daughter, Lynn, in Gardena, California, is also a Habitat supporter. Following the motto "Live simply, that others may simply live," Lynn managed twice in five years to give her father an overseas Habitat house for Christmas, and in the months between to pay for five more houses!

In October of 1985 I asked Rhodes to lead a workshop at the fall Habitat board meeting in New York City. His presentation was titled "Stewardship: God's Grace Working Through Our Faith." I doubt if there was anywhere a person better qualified to speak on that topic than Rhodes Thompson.

Obviously, it is not at all necessary to travel great distances in order to serve with Habitat. And when a new United States Habitat affiliate is launched, the impetus is supplied by local citizens who see a need right in front of them, and determine to do something about it.

Bob Whitford is in his fourth career. He spent seventeen years in private industry, eight more years with the federal government, and since 1981 he has been a professor at Purdue University in Lafayette, Indiana. In 1983 he became involved in Habitat for Humanity. Habitat, he says, is his fourth career!

In the spring of 1982, while he was studying to be a teacher in the Bethel Bible series, Bob discovered the rich possibilities of the Jubilee celebration. As a professor in public policy, he was attracted to the manner in which the three variables of production— land, labor, and capital—were treated by Yahweh in Leviticus 25. He began to do more biblical and theological research. The following year, Bob offered a course in the adult Sunday school of Central Presbyterian Church entitled "Yahweh-Nomics." About twenty people attended the class. Together, they worked to unravel the teachings found in the Old Testament and in the Gospel of Luke about the Jubilee and the sabbatical years.

At the same time, Habitat for Humanity was having its seventh anniversary "sabbatical celebration" in nearby Indianapolis. Two members of the host committee for this celebration, John and Sue Young, were in the "Yahweh-Nomics" class. The Youngs had also been involved with San Antonio Habitat before moving to Lafayette, and they invited Faith Lytle, a founder of the San Antonio Habitat project, to come to Lafayette to speak. Suddenly it became clear to Bob that here was an application of the Jubilee concept that was being practiced in the twentieth century. He got excited.

Soon Bob was translating his excitement into action. He mobilized others to form an ecumenical committee, and Lafayette Habitat was incorporated in June of 1984. Their first house was dedicated in November of 1985. Bob is still a professor at Purdue, but the volunteer hours he puts in with Habitat would be hard to count.

And I think he'll tell you that he finds his fourth career more rewarding than all the other three put together.

There is another category of Habitat partners which is, I'm happy to relate, growing all the time. These volunteers might be called "Habitat gypsies."

Jack and Lois Wolters are early retirees whose home base is Tryon, North Carolina. Both work faithfully for their local Habitat affiliate, Thermal Belt Habitat for Humanity. But they also spend several months each year taking their Airstream trailer (and a large dog) around the country from one Habitat project to another. At each stop they park their vehicle near the job site, stay for a week or a month (or as long as the local committee can persuade them!), and then move on.

Their contributions have included everything from laying ceramic tile to helping with a garage sale to babysitting a new homeowner's children. "All my skills have been put to use," says Lois, "including some I never knew I had!" By 1986 Jack and Lois had worked on at least twenty-three U.S. project locations, and they appeared to have no inclination to slow down.

David and Mary Joseph, from Onekama, Michigan, first came to Americus as volunteers in 1982. Since then they have worked energetically at Habitat projects in South Carolina, Tennessee, Florida, Michigan, and several times back at Americus. A particular joy for them, the Josephs say, has been the close friendships formed as they work beside the Habitat families. They delight in returning to a site after a new homeowner has settled in, and sharing the happiness. And as the number of projects expands, so does the list of places David and Mary plan to visit. They told me Habitat had become a vital part of their lives; I know the Josephs are a vital part of Habitat.

In 1981 Rita and Al Laflamme, of Laconia, New Hampshire, sold their business, a bakery which had been in their family for more than fifty years. The Laflammes made plans to relax for the rest of their lives. They took their motor home on the road, stopping in Americus to pay a visit to Rita's brother, Paul DuPont, who was then our building crew foreman. Al, who said he had never driven a nail in his life, started working with Paul. He liked it. Then he and Rita visited some of the awful "shotgun" shacks of the families whose homes they were working on, and that settled it. The Laflammes ended up staying in Americus for a month, and then they went on to work for varying lengths of time on Habitat projects in half a dozen other states.

Each one of these wonderful partners contracted a case of what Roger and Barbara Cross call "Habititis." Roger and Barbara are Habitat gypsies who travel between the projects in Rochester, New York, and Immokalee, Florida, having long since made themselves invaluable at both places. The only relief for Habititis, says Roger, is to continually put more love into more mortar joints. And so they do.

These roving Habitat volunteers all speak glowingly of the experiences they have shared, and the friendships they now cherish, as they travel the countryside building for God's needy children. Lois Wolters puts it this way: "Habitat is the highest paying job I have ever had!"

Lois' comment underlines an important truth: the greatest gift we can ever give anyone, rich or poor, is the gift of a vision. And when Habitat people, volunteers and homeowners alike, catch the vision of what love and service in the name of Christ can accomplish, there is no stopping them.

Gary and Linda Bergh decided in 1982 to resign from the church he pastored in upstate New York. Along with their two children, they came to Americus to spend a year in volunteer service. Throughout that time, the Berghs said, they just kept growing, as they discovered "the power that is possible through the efforts and dreams of people of faith working together." At the close of their year with us, Gary accepted a United Methodist pastorate in Malone, New York, near the Canadian border. The Berghs took their dreams with them. Two years later a new affiliate project, North Country Habitat for Humanity, was launched in Malone, and as support for the effort grew, Gary and Linda told me with certainty that "the Habitat ministry and spirit are going to make a difference in people's lives in northern New York."

Kattie Alford, of Kalamazoo, Michigan, became a Habitat home-owner in February 1986. Kattie, who worked a night job at a factory, had by day been a faithful co-worker on her house every step of the way. Often she brought her three children to clean and paint after school. But she had no intention of quitting after she moved in. Kattie, too, had caught the vision. She shared her exuberance about this partnership with everyone she met, and long before she moved in she volunteered eagerly to work on the next building: "Any house that Habitat has in the future—*I'll help!*"

Whenever Habitat people catch the vision, they immediately begin to pass it on to others. Oscar and Lydia Berger of Freeland-ville, Indiana, and Dale and Jan Christner of Ironton, Ohio, did this faithfully. Between them, over several years, these two couples led a dozen workcamps to Americus. Each time they came, they brought several veteran work campers, as well as new recruits. And they always came bearing gifts.

In 1985, Dale and Jan were instrumental in forming the Ashland-Ironton Area Habitat for Humanity, serving neighboring cities in Kentucky and Ohio. Shortly thereafter Jan began intensive training for our one-thousand-mile walk to Kansas City in 1986.

George Anderson, director of Faith at Work, Canada, traveled to Haiti in 1984 to help build a Habitat house. He came home so thrilled with the opportunities for service which he had experi-enced that he caught a vision for his entire country!

George began to raise funds and organize Haiti work camps from all across Canada. Seven groups had made that trip by early 1986, and plans were underway for other work trips to Haiti and to Central and South America, as well as to United States projects. He also brought four volunteers to join the 1985 Lower East Side work week led by President Carter. In dozens of speaking engage-ments around his country, George shared his dream—that Canada might become the second Western nation to develop a Habitat ministry on a large scale. That dream began to take shape at our fall 1985 board meeting, when the first Habitat national center outside the United States was approved: Habitat for Humanity of Canada, Inc.

John Pritchard, of Kansas City, Missouri, is treasurer of our Habitat board of directors and founder of the project in Kansas City. A successful businessman who holds degrees from both Princeton and Harvard, John chose semi-retirement in 1979 in order to devote nearly all his energies to Habitat. In 1982 he and his wife, Mary, traveled with Linda and me to visit Habitat projects and proposed sites in Papua New Guinea, Pakistan, Kenya, Uganda, and Zaire. The unforgettable people we encountered, and the shocking needs we surveyed, created within all of us a renewed determination to expand Habitat's work.

At the last stop, en route home from our long journey, we had been asked to speak at the American Protestant Church of the Hague, Holland. John's brief presentation, at the close of the program, was filled with emotion. He and Mary, he said, had just completed the most remarkable trip they had ever experienced. Then he concluded his talk with a powerful statement I will always remember.

"I've spent much of my life," John said, "building second homes for the rich. I intend to spend the remainder of my life building first homes for the poor."

Habitat volunteers come in all sizes, ages, colors, and skill levels. If you should decide to make a commitment of your time and resources to helping God's people have a decent place to live, you may be sure we have a job for you.[1]

But if you plan on real involvement, be forewarned. It will change your life.

---

1   The volunteer program of Habitat for Humanity is guided by the Director of Volunteer Services. This position was assumed in 1985 by Diane Nunne-lee, a United Methodist campus minister from Springfield, Missouri. Persons or groups interested in volunteering should write to Director of Volunteer Services, Habitat for Humanity, Habitat and Church Streets, Americus, Georgia 31709, or contact your nearest Habitat affiliate or regional center. See Appendix C for a full listing of these addresses.

9

The Theology of the Hammer

There is no doubt about it. The resources, both material and human, sufficient to house everybody already exist. Building materials in an abundant variety are scattered over the earth. It is true that in some places the necessary supplies are not immediately adjacent to a particular construction site. It is also true that extra creativity may be required in order to build in some areas. But adequate materials of one kind or another are available.

Furthermore, there is enough money in the world to house everybody. Not in mansions. Not in opulent villas with saunas, swimming pools, and tennis courts. But simple, decent houses can be built for *every* family. There is enough money for that.

Human resources are also in ample supply. Millions of people on this earth already know how to saw boards, mix mortar, lay blocks, put on roofing, drive nails. They know how to build a house! That's no big technological feat. Some people in this scientific age know how to construct living quarters that will rise straight up from the ground and go to the moon, and beyond. Other structures need no foundation at all—they simply float endlessly in space. So building a simple house on a conventional foundation is really a snap.

In addition, new kinds of resources for housing the burgeoning population of the world are available, or can be made available, as the need arises. Ingenuity and dedication will both be required. But we do not face an impossible task.

John E. Cox, former director of the International Year of Shelter for the Homeless, United Nations Centre for Human Settlements, wrote an article in the July/August 1984 issue of *Ekistics*. (Taking its name from a Greek word for the problems and science of human settlements, *Ekistics* researches international needs and trends in providing shelter. The magazine is published in Greece by the Athens Technological Organization.) In his article, Mr. Cox outlined the massive challenge of housing the world's poor, gave a seven-point strategy for solving the problem, and then concluded with this startlingly positive statement: *"It is our sincere belief that the problem of shelter for the poor is soluble, and that it can be solved before the end of this century."*

I confess that I am skeptical about Mr. Cox's timetable. There may still be people living in pitiful conditions in the year 2000, no matter how much is done. But vast progress can unquestionably be made by that time. To accomplish this objective, however, attitudes toward the poor must be drastically changed; and the creative genius of humankind must be focused on the challenge of housing all of God's people.

Some inventive approaches to house building are already being pioneered in Japan. Sekisui Heim is a company with six factories mass-producing houses the way Toyota builds cars. Utilizing computers to design individualized houses, room size components are fabricated, largely by robots, at a factory and then transported to the home site. This company puts up a house every forty-four minutes.

The second largest prefab home builder in Japan is Misawa Homes. The president of this company, Chiyoji Misawa, believes that the materials of the future in home building are silicon and ceramics. Silicon is extracted from common sand; ceramics are made from sand and clay. Already marketing the world's first ceramic house, Misawa Homes molds the exterior from a building material called PALC (precastable autoclaved lightweight ceramics). PALC is made from silica and limestone, both of which are dug from a hillside near the factory.

Prefabricating homes for the poor has been pioneered by an organization in Colombia, South America, called Servivienda, or—roughly translated—The Low-Cost Housing Service Foundation. I visited the main production facility of this group in 1978. Headquartered in Bogotá, the capital, Servivienda was founded by Father Alberto Jimenez Cadena, a Roman Catholic priest. Panels of thin concrete are mass produced in a central location and then trucked to the building site. The recipient family must already have prepared the site and poured a concrete slab floor; then their entire house can be erected in a few hours.

It is clear that the resources and technology are available for building on an enormous scale. Why then are so many people still living in miserable, sub-human conditions? The answer, I think, is simply that *the will to solve the problem is too weak*.

Dr. Arcot Ramachandran, Undersecretary-General and Executive Director of the United Nations Centre for Human Settlements, in an address to the International Shelter Conference in Washington, D.C., on November 2, 1984, challenged the real estate profession to help solve the world's shelter problems. After stating that no group is better placed to understand the situation and hence to contribute to a practical solution, he posed a series of questions:

Are the realtors not, among other things, experienced in identifying, assembling, and preparing land for development? Are they not transferring plots and dealing with related legal questions? And are they not arranging investment support and financial backing for all sorts of development schemes? As governments in many countries plan massive interventions in the land market in trying to meet the needs of ever-growing city populations, could not real estate professionals take the initiative and give advice and practical assistance towards solving the land-tenure problems of the poor, whose situation verges on the catastrophic? Could they not devise large-scale, economical and efficient operations to provide land for housing low-income groups?

Dr. Ramachandran then answered his own questions:

They have the knowledge and experience; all they require is the desire and the will to invoke these, the vision and commitment to do in an innovative way what they have always done best—render a service to those in quest of shelter.

Other groups and individuals in society could also make significant contributions toward helping the poor have at least a simple, decent place to live and raise their families. It is indeed a matter of will and desire.

In the United States many private organizations, in addition to Habitat for Humanity, are working to solve the housing crisis. Two that are doing significant work are the Enterprise Foundation and the Nehemiah Plan. The former group grew out of the Jubilee Housing Program of the Church of the Savior in Washington, D.C. Founded by the nationally known developer James Rouse, and headquartered in Columbia, Maryland, the Enterprise Foundation had projects in twenty-five cities by 1986. Their most ambitious program is under way in Chattanooga, Tennessee, where their objective is the elimination of sub-standard housing by the year 1995.

The goal of the Enterprise Foundation, states Rouse, is "not simply to work at the problems of housing the very poor but, along with others, to see that they are solved, and see that the poor are adequately housed within a generation."

The Nehemiah Plan was organized in 1980 by East Brooklyn Churches, a coalition of fifty congregations, to revive battered neighborhoods in Brooklyn. Their project envisions building more than five thousand houses in the eastern part of the borough. Six years after their founding, the group had completed over three hundred houses on land donated by the city. These houses were sold at cost (a little over $50,000), with New York City providing $10,000 grants plus tax abatements, to be repaid immediately if the houses are resold. Purchasers pay $5,000 down and receive a below-market interest rate mortgage from New York State for the balance. Needless to say, this program is not for the very poor, but it does enable families who cannot qualify for conventional financing to acquire adequate housing on terms they can afford.

Church World Service, the Mennonite Central Committee, the United Methodist Committee on Relief, and many other church-related organizations are also engaged in efforts to alleviate the worldwide housing crisis. Creative Ministries, headquartered in Columbia, Missouri, is an agency of the United Methodist Church which has a special concern for the poor of third world countries. This program has developed a little transportable house for refugees. As this book goes to press, the house is being field-tested in Central America.

Many secular agencies are also working on the need for low-cost shelter. The Cooperative Housing Foundation, headquartered in Washington, D.C., has since 1952 been involved in planning and developing low-income housing programs in the United States and abroad. They also push for a national commitment to the goal of decent homes for all Americans. Experimenting currently with adobe, or sun-dried brick, this group hopes to improve technical methods of earth construction in ways that will make simple houses both durable and affordable.

The foundation collaborates in the development of this technology with the International Foundation for Earth Construction. IFEC sees adobe as a primary source of inexpensive, low-maintenance, earthquake-resistant building materials, and works on facilitating the production of improved earth bricks using stabilizers such as cement, lime, or petroleum to make them water-resistant. They also study methods, still more economical, of coating existing adobe houses with stabilized adobe, thus extending the structures' useful life almost indefinitely. In Fresno, California, the Hans Sumpf Company markets a technique called "Asfadobe," which has been widely used to stabilize earth bricks for nearly fifty years. More recently, a computerized machine has been developed in Lawrenceburg, Tennessee, which uses ordinary earth, under pressures up to 1,875 pounds per square inch, to produce durable building blocks. These "terrablocks" are turned out at the rate of six to ten per minute, and can be dry-stacked without mortar if the foundation is suitably leveled.

But the combined efforts of all these private organizations and all the government housing programs currently in operation around the world are not nearly enough. We face a catastrophe of the first magnitude, and these groups are barely putting a Band-aid on it.

As a Christian, I believe that a willingness to allow millions of people, all of whom are made in the image of God, to exist in utter misery is an outward sign of an inner sickness. This problem will be solved only when we probe deeply into our spiritual selves and open up our souls to the healing hand of God. Too many people who have been blessed with great talents and abilities are using those God-endowed gifts only for their own selfish interests. Such folks urgently need to hear again the powerful voice of Isaiah:

> The Lord says, "Let my people return to me. Remove every obstacle from their path! Build the road and make it ready! I am the high and holy God, who lives forever. I live in a high and holy place, but I also live with people who are humble and repentant, so that I can restore their confidence and hope. . . . I was angry with them because of their sin and greed, and so I punished them and abandoned them. But they were stubborn and kept on going their own way. I have seen how they acted, but I will heal them. I will lead them and help them, and I will comfort those who mourn. I offer peace to all, both near and far! I will heal my people (Isa. 57:14–19).

God wants His people to turn away from sin and greed and stubborn selfishness. He pleads for a people who are humble and repentant. We are told to "Return . . . remove every obstacle . . . build!" When we live that way, God promises to restore confidence and hope, to heal our deepest illness. And peace will come.

For any who choose to turn away unheeding, Isaiah continues to deliver his stern message directly from the Lord:

> Shout as loud as you can! Tell my people about their sins! . . . You pursue your own interests and oppress your workers. Your fasting makes you violent, and you quarrel and fight. Do you think this kind of fasting will make me listen to your prayers? . . . The kind of fasting I want is this: Remove the chains of oppression and the yoke of injustice, and let the oppressed go free. Share your food with the hungry, and open your homes to the homeless poor. Give clothes to those who have nothing to wear, and do not refuse to help your own relatives. . . . If you put an end to oppression, to every gesture of contempt, and to every evil word; if you give food

to the hungry and satisfy those who are in need, then the darkness around you will turn to the brightness of noon. And I will always guide you and satisfy you with good things. I will keep you strong and well. You will be like a garden that has plenty of water, like a spring of water that never goes dry. Your people will rebuild what has long been in ruins, building again on the old foundations. You will be known as the people who rebuilt the walls, who restored the ruined houses (Isa. 58:1–12).

Throughout the pages of Scripture, God is revealed as a loving Father who wants *all* of His people to share in the good things of life. And, as Isaiah announces with memorable eloquence, those who are in a position to help the poor and oppressed are under specific orders from above to do so.

Again and again, stern biblical warnings are issued concerning the awful consequences of forgetting the Lord's instructions about the needy. Moses had special words of caution for people who become wealthy:

Make certain that you do not forget the Lord your God; do not fail to obey any of his laws that I am giving you today. When you have all you want to eat and have built good houses to live in and when your cattle and sheep, your silver and gold, and all your other possessions have increased, be sure that you do not become proud and forget the Lord your God. . . . You must never think that you made yourselves wealthy by your own power and strength. Remember that it is the Lord your God who gives you the power to become rich. . . . Never forget the Lord your God or turn to other gods to worship and serve them. If you do, then I warn you today that you will certainly be destroyed (Deut. 8:11–14, 17–19).

The prophet Amos lived in a time of great prosperity, a feeling of national security and notable religious piety. But Amos was painfully aware that the prosperity was sustained by injustice; the security was more apparent than real; and religious observances were strictly for show. And he had some dire words for the wealthy in the northern kingdom of Israel:

How terrible it will be for you that stretch out on your luxurious couches, feasting on veal and lamb! You like to compose songs, as

David did, and play them on harps. You drink wine by the bowlful and use the finest perfumes, but you do not mourn over the ruin of Israel. So you will be the first to go into exile. Your feasts and banquets will come to an end. The Sovereign Lord Almighty has given this solemn warning: "I hate the pride of the people. . . . I despise their luxurious mansions. I will give their capital city and everything in it to the enemy" (Amos 6:4–8).

Does this sound relevant to our situation? A privileged few in our day bask in luxury, while millions of people don't even have the basic necessities of life. Who will be concerned *to the point of action* to help those who don't have the veal and lamb, or luxurious couches and the finest perfumes—or even a house to live in? Amos admonishes all of us:

> Make it your aim to do what is right, not what is evil, so that you may live. Then the Lord God Almighty really will be with you, as you claim he is. Hate what is evil, love what is right. . . . Perhaps the Lord will be merciful to the people of this nation who are still left alive (Amos 5:14–15).

John the Baptist, in his day, minced no words when he was approached by people who wanted to be baptized. Getting dunked by a preacher is definitely not sufficient, he told them.

> "You snakes," he shouted, "Who told you that you could escape from the punishment God is about to send? Do those things that will show that you have turned from your sins. . . . The axe is ready to cut down the trees at the roots; every tree that does not bear good fruit will be cut down and thrown in the fire." The people asked him, "What are we to do, then?" He answered, "Whoever has two shirts must give one to the man who has none, and whoever has food must share it" (Luke 3:7–11).

You *must* share, John the Baptist exclaimed. This is true religion. Lifting others up. Bringing the poor to a better life. Doing things that show a broken and a contrite heart. Then the world sees, and not just hears, that you have turned from your selfish, sinful life.

Throughout the Bible, service to the Lord and help for the poor are tied together. In Deuteronomy we read,

I command you, saying, You shall freely open your hand to your brother, to your needy and poor in your land. (Deut. 15:11, NASB).

In Matthew's Gospel, Jesus makes the connection very personal.

"I was hungry and you fed me, thirsty and you gave me a drink; I was a stranger and you received me in your homes, naked and you clothed me; I was sick and you took care of me, in prison and you visited me." The righteous will then answer him, "When, Lord, did we ever see you hungry and feed you, or thirsty and give you a drink? When did we ever see you a stranger and welcome you in our homes, or naked and clothe you? When did we ever see you sick or in prison, and visit you?" The King will reply, "I tell you, whenever you did this for one of the least important of these brothers of mine, you did it for me!" (Matt. 25:35–40).

In God's sight, looking pious and sounding religious are totally inadequate.

Not everyone who calls me "Lord, Lord," will enter the kingdom of heaven; but only those who do what my Father in heaven wants them to do (Matt. 7:21).

Furthermore, whenever we sincerely reach out a helping hand to the poor, we must do more than just drop a few crumbs at their feet. God expects us to share from our substance.

Jesus looked around and saw rich men dropping their gifts in the temple treasury, and he also saw a very poor widow dropping in two little copper coins. He said, "I tell you that this poor widow put in more than all the others. For the others offered their gifts from what they had to spare of their riches; but she, poor as she is, gave all she had to live on" (Luke 21:1–4).

The most powerful—and frightening—story in all of Scripture, about the judgment of God on the rich who do not share with the poor in a significant way, is the one Jesus told about the rich man and Lazarus. It is recorded in the sixteenth chapter of Luke. The rich man, Jesus said, "dressed in the most expensive clothes, and lived in great luxury every day." Who was this rich man? We don't know for sure, but I am quite positive he was well known about town. He probably owned several businesses, or perhaps he was a famous sports personality or a popular entertainer. He may have "married well." In any event, he had it made. Surely he lived in a palatial home and had several vacation cottages as well. Undoubtedly his table was always laden with sumptuous foods. Everybody knew him. Indeed, it was impossible not to know him. He was somebody important!

On the other hand, a certain beggar lay at the gate of the rich man's big house. The beggar was alone. No one knew him. No one cared to know him. He was an unimportant man, and his name was not spoken about town. He was an absolute nobody.

But notice something about this remarkable story. Because Jesus tells it from God's point of view, the rich man has no name. He is only "a rich man." The poor man, on the other hand, has a name. He is Lazarus, a person known and loved by the Lord.

There is another dynamite dimension to this story which is easily missed. The rich man was actually a concerned person! He had been regularly feeding Lazarus some leftovers from his bounteous table. How can I be sure? Because I've had stray dogs and cats show up at our door, and I know that they don't keep coming back unless you give them at least *something*. The rich man, when he had eaten all he wanted, was having his servants throw a few scraps over the fence to poor Lazarus. He could just as easily have dumped the scraps into a hole in the ground. In fact, if he had done that the poor beggar wouldn't have kept coming back to clutter up his beautiful landscape. But the rich man was undoubtedly concerned. His concern was simply limited. It did not extend beyond giving away a few scraps from his excess.

How did God reward such concern? The account in Luke is graphic. "The rich man died and went to hell."

The poignancy of this powerful tale was brought home to me recently, when I received a phone call from a wealthy, socially prominent woman in Americus. The conversation began abruptly. She questioned why we weren't working on the house for Dorothy.

"Dorothy who?" I asked.

"You know—Dorothy."

I told her that I knew several Dorothys. "Which Dorothy?"

"My maid who has been with me for eight years—Dorothy!"

I tried again. "Do you know her last name?"

The woman sputtered, "The Dorothy who lives down near your office."

"Oh, *that* Dorothy!" I exclaimed.

"Now," she asked again, "why have you stopped building her house?"

I informed my caller that the construction on Dorothy's house was only temporarily stalled. But when I reminded her that it takes money to build houses, and suggested that her contribution could speed up progress on Dorothy's house, she became very indignant. This woman was concerned just enough to call about her maid's housing conditions. She did not care enough to help substantively.

What is the extent of your concern for the poor? Are you so concerned that God knows your name? Or are you just another rich man or woman, well known among your contemporaries, but a person without a name in God's kingdom? Do you share with others in a substantial, sacrificial way? Or does your concern begin only when your own wants and desires are completely fulfilled? Jesus reminds us: "God knows your hearts . . . the things that are considered of great value by man are worth nothing in God's sight."* As God's people, we must be concerned about every Lazarus and every Dorothy in our world. And that concern must go beyond casual talking and scraps of giving. It must result in significant gifts and in purposeful actions which change things.

Jesus launched his ministry with a bold proclamation: He had been chosen to bring good news to the poor. Throughout the next three years He preached this good news of eternal salvation, available through Him to all who believe. But He also delivered good news to the poor in the form of food for the hungry, health for the sick, sight for the blind, a right mind for the spiritually tortured and even life for the dead. At the same time, those who were wealthy were consistently admonished to share what they had with those who had little. After meeting Jesus, Zacchaeus gave half of his belongings to the poor.† Jesus asked the rich young ruler for *all* of his money—for the poor.‡ On still another occasion,

* Luke 16:15
† Luke 19:8
‡ Luke 18:22

in order to help His listeners avoid "every kind of greed," Jesus told the story about a rich landowner who decided to build bigger barns for storing his enlarging wealth. He wasn't going to share his hard-earned gain. Like all rich men, sooner or later he would die and leave his wealth to someone else. But in his case it was sooner. And God said to him, "You fool!"*

The early Christians, those followers who were closest to Jesus in time, obviously understood his message, for they generously shared with the needy. In Acts, Luke reports that:

> Those who owned fields or houses would sell them, bring the money received from the sale, and turn it over to the apostles; and the money was distributed to each one according to his need (Acts 4:34–35).

The Apostle Paul wrote very specifically on the subject of sharing with the poor.

> I am not trying to relieve others by putting a burden on you; but since you have plenty at this time, it is only fair that you should help those who are in need. Then, when you are in need and they have plenty, they will help you. In this way both are treated equally. As the Scripture says, "The one who gathered much did not have too much, and the one who gathered little did not have too little" (2 Cor. 8:13–15).

The life of a Christian should be characterized by a joyous abandon about possessions. We can and should enjoy material things, but only in a shared sense, with the full knowledge that we cannot truly own anything, since the earth is the Lord's and the fullness thereof. If we are to love our neighbor as we love ourselves, we must be as aware of our neighbor's need as we are of our own, and as ready to share with that neighbor as we are to do something for ourselves.

By His teaching and His example, Jesus gave the world a clear picture of the kingdom of heaven. Indeed, I think Jesus and His disciples constituted a microcosm of that Kingdom. They shared totally with one another. Jesus was their Lord and Master and yet an intimate friend. He served them in such a complete way

* Luke 12:15–20

that He washed their feet and commanded them to do the same for each other. He also taught them an unconditional love for everyone, even opponents and mortal enemies. Then, after teaching them what the kingdom was like, He taught them to pray, "Thy kingdom come; Thy will be done on earth as it is in heaven."*

When you pray this prayer today, do you realize what you are asking for? Apply this portion of the Lord's prayer to possessions. Do you think there will be rich and poor in heaven? Is it God's will for some people to have so much to eat that they constantly worry about being overweight, while others don't even have scraps from the table sufficient to sustain life? Can you conceive of a heavenly kingdom in which some favored folks bask eternally in opulence, while others languish in hell holes of indescribable poverty?

I cannot. And every time I pray that prayer I am motivated anew to work with all the energy I can muster, as a vital part of God's kingdom on earth, to make it as it is in heaven.

On one occasion Jesus commented explicitly on the matter of shelter in the kingdom.

> There are many rooms in my Father's house, and I am going to prepare a place for you. I would not tell you this if it were not so. And after I go and prepare a place for you, I will come back and take you to myself, so that you will be where I am (John 14:2–3).

I have heard this Scripture read solemnly at many funerals, and surely it is appropriate at such times. Jesus has prepared a place for His people on the other side. Such assurance to the family of a departed loved one is comforting. However, restricting this Scripture solely to such occasions and for such a purpose misses the main point of Jesus' sharing this kingdom news with His disciples.

Remember that God is a God of the living.† Jesus was going to leave His disciples for a while, but they had to remain in the world. The main point of Jesus' telling His followers about their house on the other side was to set their minds at ease on that subject. He was in charge of the Habitat project in heaven, so to

* Matthew 6:10
† Matthew 22:32

speak. Perfect dwelling places were going up for His followers, so they wouldn't have to worry another minute about that. He wanted them—and us—to concentrate every bit of living energy on being His faithful representatives on earth.

Listen to the startling promises Jesus made to the disciples immediately following His assurances concerning their heavenly home:

> Whoever believes in me will do what I do—yes, he will do even greater things, because I am going to the Father. And I will do whatever you ask for in my name, so that the Father's glory will be shown through the Son. If you ask me for anything in my name, I will do it (John 14:12–14).

In chapter fifteen of John's Gospel the promise is repeated twice more to the believers: *Ask for anything and it will be done.* The disciples are instructed to abide in Jesus, and then God's glory will be shown by their bearing much fruit.

Do you believe in Jesus? If so, this promise extends to you. Greater works than Jesus did shall you do. Can you imagine anything more fantastic? More incredible? Ask Jesus for anything, in His name, and He will do it. We are told to ask, and if we abide in Him, our asking will always be such that we are constantly extending the kingdom. We are appointed to be fruit bearers for Christ in the heavenly kingdom on earth.

Jesus further says that we are to bear "the kind of fruit that endures."* And one of the fruits we are called to produce is decent living conditions for those who don't have them. God has already told us, through the prophet Isaiah, that the religious observance or "fast" which is pleasing to him involves inviting the stranger in. Jesus repeats the message, and equates issuing the invitation to inviting Him personally into our homes. Habitat for Humanity is creatively "inviting the stranger in." We are building houses for these "strangers" so that they too can share in the joyous experience of inviting still other strangers into their homes.

Life is a mystery, and there is much we don't understand. I believe, however, that life does have a purpose. I further believe that God has called me, as he calls others, to enter into the joy of sharing and serving in His name. A significant part of my calling,

* John 15:16

and I hope yours, is to join a growing host of concerned people to build, renovate and repair houses for God's needy people throughout the world.

In Habitat for Humanity we have gathered all these biblical teachings about the poor into "the theology of the hammer." This simply means that as Christians we will agree on the use of the hammer as an instrument to manifest God's love. We may disagree on all sorts of other things—baptism, communion, what night to have prayer meeting, and how the preacher should dress—but we can agree on the imperative of the gospel to serve others in the name of the Lord. We can agree on the idea of building houses for God's people in need, and on doing so using Biblical economics: no profit and no interest.[1]

In August 1985 I was impressed to read an address given by Pope John Paul II at the United Nations office in Nairobi, Kenya. Referring to the work of the U.N. Centre for Human Settlements, the pope recalled the words of Jesus: "Foxes have holes, and birds of the air have nests, but the Son of Man has nowhere to lay His head."* And he appealed for international assistance and solidarity in order to provide food and shelter for the poor.

> We see in the faces of the homeless the face of Christ the Lord, and we feel impelled, by love of Him and by His example of generous self-giving, to seek to do everything we can to help those living in conditions unworthy of their human dignity. At the same time, we gladly join hands with all people of good will, in the worthy efforts being made to provide adequate housing for the millions of people in today's world who are living in absolute destitution. . . . In the words of Pope Paul VI, "Development is the new name for peace" . . . and programs for food and housing [are] the concrete way of promoting peace. Peace is built slowly, through good will, trust, and persevering effort. It is built by international agencies and by governmental and non-governmental organizations, when they engage in common efforts to provide food and shelter for the needy, and when they work together to improve the environment.

The biblical command to share our possessions, time and ideas with the poor is clear. It is not an option. It is a requirement.

---

* Matthew 8:20

Furthermore, cooperating as God's people, building together in spite of philosophical or theological differences, is right, and absolutely necessary.

We've discussed our theology. And we've agreed to work together to demonstrate God's love.

Now let's go get our hammers.

---

1   A full discussion of biblical economics is found in chapter 8 of *Love in the Mortar Joints*, entitled "The Economics of Jesus."

Manhatten's Lower East Side: Jimmy Carter at the renovation site with a local resident *(left)*. Rosalynn Carter drives nails with another Habitat volunteer *(right)*.

ight: Jimmy Carter
nd other workers
epair the inside of the
9-unit dwelling.

Left: Run-down, hazardous apartment building on the Lower East Side. Right: President Carter speaks at the dedication of the newly renovated building.

Left: Volunteer workers restore a house in Salem County, New Jersey.

Above: Norma Ueleke shoveling sand alongside national workers in Kikwit, Zaire. (Photo by Bill Moore.) Right: Hugh O'Brien mixing cement in Nzoia, Kenya.

Left: Volunteers in Americus, Georgia.

Right: Workers on the Habitat project in Baltimore, Maryland.

Left: Mississippi State Penitentiary inmate Tommy Allen donates his time to help build housing for the poverty-stricken in the Mississippi Delta area.

Right: Members of the 1984 Overseas Volunteer Orientation class.

Left: Sub-standard poverty housing commonly found throughout the Mississippi Delta.

Right: Using "Jesus economics" to build new homes for needy families.

Above: Stan Bright, president of the Habitat affiliate in Sumner, Mississippi, and Luther Millsaps, executive director of Habitat South. Right: Collecting cans to raise funds for Greene County Habitat's projects in Pennsylvania.

10

The Crazy Idea Works

Habitat for Humanity is a crazy idea. Skeptics, many of them professing Christians, continue to insist that selling houses at no profit to low-income people, charging no interest, undertaking construction projects worldwide without government money, and expecting thousands of volunteers to give weeks or months or years of their lives to work for practically nothing—all these are crazy ideas. But these are God's ideas, solidly based on biblical commands and promises. And, like a lot of other instructions He gave to people like Noah and Joshua and David and Gideon—messages which seemed pretty crazy at the time—they work.

Furthermore, what never ceases to confound these skeptics is that Habitat's unlikely methods will work anywhere in the world. Differences in culture and language and economic system cannot obscure a universal truth: Everyone wants and needs decent shelter. And whatever the location, when people band together to build with God's ideas, their efforts will succeed.

Let me take you on a quick tour of some places where this has happened.

Zenon Colque Rojas, the Peruvian engineer who walked to Indianapolis with us, came to New Mexico in 1981 to work on a solar energy project. A friend told him about Habitat for Humanity, and he caught the vision of a partnership housing program for his countrymen. The vision has been enlarging ever since. It started in the city of Puno, in the Andes Mountains of southern Peru on the shores of Lake Titicaca (the highest navigable lake in the world—more than two miles above sea level). Then the work expanded to the nearby village of Manazo, and later to the neighboring city of Juliaca. Hundreds of people in this area now live for the first time in decent homes, and the project keeps growing.

In 1984 volunteer Ken Van Dyke, of Grand Rapids, Michigan, wrote us a letter about what was happening in Puno.

> Agustin Llanque, a short, bouncy man with a boyish face, reminds me of a dancing bear. One day he came to my desk and stood there as if he had business—which is what I expected, since he is in charge of our warehouse. Then he broke into a wide grin: "Mister Kenny, they're putting the roof on *my* house today!" All he really wanted was someone to share his excitement.
>
> There are over one hundred families in the Puno Habitat Association. All of them in some way personify the spirit of Habitat, but to me—perhaps because I see them so often—Agustin's family is special. For five years Agustin, with his wife and five children, lived in one rented room of a two-room adobe house in Puno, without water or sanitary facilities. Often Agustin had to leave home to seek work in other villages. In 1983 they joined the Habitat Association, and Agustin came to work for us. For six months they lived in an adobe hut on the project site, guarding the materials and homes. During the rainy season their floor was flooded. When we put up the shell of the home that is serving temporarily as our storage building, the Llanques moved into the back bedroom. When they moved into their permanent home late in November, they were the seventeenth family to receive a Habitat home at this site.
>
> The Llanques's home is 470 square feet, with two bedrooms, a dining/living area, a kitchen, and a bath. The bath will serve as

storage for a while, since we do not yet have sewage and running water to the homes. We do have a twenty-thousand-gallon spring-fed cistern, water main piping in the streets, and community latrines, a marked improvement over the conditions in many of the barrios of Puno. Someday we will have running water, sewage, electricity, a school and playground, and a commercial area. We are building for the future, leveling hills on this fifteen-acre site, laying out and compacting streets, and lining them with young trees.

My family needs no alarm clock here. Every morning at sunrise we awaken to the sound of wheelbarrows: Habitat families on the way to build their new community. There are no lazy people in this project. There are a great many brothers and sisters who—like you—believe in the Habitat vision and give of themselves to make it come true.

Laboring together on the Peru Habitat project have been local Roman Catholics as well as American missionary nuns from Cincinnati; local Seventh Day Adventists; and American volunteers from the Church of the Brethren, Christian Reformed, Roman Catholic and United Methodist Churches.

Does "the theology of the hammer" sound crazy? It works.

When Art Russell, of Glenwood, New Mexico, went to Dumay, Haiti, in 1982 to launch the Habitat project there, his first letter home sent me scurrying to my dictionary. He described the pitiful houses the people of the village lived in as "scrofulous." I studied the definitions: (1) resembling a tuberculous disease of the lymph glands; or (2) morally contaminated.

When I visited Dumay a few months later, I knew that Art's adjective was precisely the right one. The houses were horrible.

The poverty around Dumay, in fact, was so great that it was almost impossible to find anyone who did not qualify for a new house. Therefore a lottery system was instituted to choose the families. Eligible names were put in a box and stirred up; then fifty were chosen to receive the first fifty houses. As additional volunteers and support arrived in Haiti, the simple houses (387 square feet, consisting of two bedrooms and a living area, plus a covered porch of 75 square feet) began going up steadily, almost at the rate of one a week. Later another fifty-family lottery was held.

The average income of the villagers who became homeowners under this system was no more than $500 *per year*, and doubters would certainly say that no one living at that level could possibly buy any kind of a house. In Dumay, scores of families have already done just that. Their homes cost approximately $1500 to build, with an additional $100 for an outdoor latrine. Their twenty-year mortgage payments are about $80 per year.

The effort to meet even such minimal payments has been a real struggle for most of the villagers. But they are succeeding. And moving from scrofulous to solid and safe is bringing joyful thanksgiving to new homeowners in Dumay.

In Khammam, in southern India, Roger and Barbara Sneller and their two small daughters, of Zeeland, Michigan, teamed up with Korabanda Azariah Rajasekhorarao (known, fortunately for us, as Mr. Azariah) to launch a Habitat project. Roger and Barbara, who earlier served a year in water, sanitation, and health programs with the Peace Corps in Oman, decided in 1983 to volunteer two years with Habitat's first project in India.

Mr. Azariah was a Cambridge-educated evangelist of the Church of South India, who worked with village pastors, hospital patients, and a home for the elderly. When he heard about Habitat, he determined to bring a Christian housing program to poor families in his area as well.

There are more than two hundred thousand people in Khammam. In the neighborhood where Habitat began building, the families earned an average of $300 per year. According to their income, families chose a house with two rooms and a covered porch for $830, or one with three rooms and a covered porch for $1450.

As the project continued, not only the families helped in hauling rocks and making bricks. Word got around about this new venture, and an encouraging amount of community involvement began to develop. Teenagers from a Sunday school at St. Mary's Church of South India came to help dig foundations; then eight college students showed up to dig some more. On another day a troop of Khammam Boy Scouts appeared, forming a human chain to transport mortar fifty yards up a hill where a truck could not go.

In a land where the need is so great, it was exciting to see the vision enlarging.

When David Rowe was in Khammam in 1985 for the dedication of the first sixteen homes there, he was thrilled. The new houses were beautiful, and presented a welcome feeling of permanence, among rows of shanties in all stages of sad disrepair. The atmosphere throughout the development was cheerful and clean, in contrast to the squalor around it.

A government official approached David at the dedication to inquire how Habitat for Humanity could build better houses than anyone else, for less cost. David grinned. "We use *love* in the mortar joints," he replied.

That statement required some elaboration. A Christian attempting to explain the economics of Jesus to a Muslim in a Hindu country must choose his words carefully. By the time he had finished, said David, "I think he had a sense that something is going on there in Khammam beyond just building houses."

And perhaps, if we continue faithfully building and praying, that government official will really come to understand why our crazy idea works.

Habitat follows another significant biblical teaching which the world generally regards as utterly crazy. We believe in tithing.

From the earliest Old Testament times we have been instructed that the first tenth of everything we have belongs to the Lord,* and is to be shared with "the foreigners, orphans, and widows who live in your towns. They are to come and get all they need. Do this, and the LORD your God will bless you in everything you do."† Habitat folks know that tithing does indeed result in abundant blessings.

The wonderful thing about tithing is that it never stops giving. Many Habitat supporters dedicate a tithe of their monthly mortgage or rent payment to help a poor family obtain a house; when those new homeowners begin making payments, the money is immediately recycled toward another house; United States Habitat affiliates

---

* Leviticus 27:30–32
† Deuteronomy 14:22, 28–29

contribute a tithe or more of their income to still needier projects overseas; and overseas projects often send a tithe of their special offerings to aid yet another Habitat program somewhere else in the world. Jesus specifically teaches that it is more blessed to give; no one, no matter how poor, should be denied that blessing.

The average cost of a Habitat house in a developing country is roughly 10 percent of a U.S. Habitat house. This means that every time a project completes a home in the United States, they have at the same time housed at least one other family overseas. Sometimes a local group will even send one of their members to the third world project where their tithe has been designated, in order to help build "their" house. And through this experience the blessings continue to multiply.

In 1985, Koinonia Partners voted to tithe all the house payments from their Partnership Housing program to the Habitat for Humanity projects in Nicaragua and Uganda. At that time Koinonia, which had been building new houses steadily for sixteen years, had completed one hundred and fifty-five homes in Sumter County. Their tithe amounted to a thousand dollars each month, and it escalated as each new family moved in. At the big "Habitation" during our fall 1985 board meeting in New York City, project representatives were asked to present their tithes. A total of over forty thousand dollars was received—*before* we took the evening offering! (Several people from the Clarkesville, Georgia, area had come to New York to attend their first board meeting in order to apply for affiliation as Habitat for Humanity of Northeast Georgia. They amazed everyone by arriving with their initial tithe already in hand, and their new president, Bo Turner, placed a check for three thousand dollars in the offering.)

Unless you've tried giving back to the Lord 10 percent—and more—of all you have received, you will be baffled to hear that tithing always brings unexpected joys. But that's the promise of Scripture. And Habitat people know it works.

All of us involved with Habitat seek to be peacemakers. We believe the Lord has called us to demonstrate His crazy ideas to those in need, wherever they are. For this reason we continue to work in countries like Guatemala, Uganda, Nicaragua, and Haiti, where the political climate is uncertain and volatile.

Obviously, the effort to maintain a visible witness for Christ in countries torn by civil strife is fraught with problems and obstacles. Sometimes it's scary.

In September of 1985, following another coup in Uganda, the army again seized Habitat's indispensable Leland dump truck. During this coup, Ugandans working on the project in Gulu had ingeniously hidden the truck several times; and occasionally workers walked eight or nine miles carrying heavy pieces of mahogany for rafters on their heads and shoulders in order to keep the construction going. But the overwhelming need to transport materials eventually persuaded the project leaders to bring the truck out of hiding, and it was promptly confiscated.

The Habitat committee decided that George Okot, the Habitat driver, would stay with the truck at the Army Motor Pool so that it would not be abused by army drivers. Three days later, loaded with soldiers and driven by George, the truck was fired on by guerillas along the road to Kampala. The windshield and rear window were shattered by bullets; the radiator, one front tire and a headlight were also hit. Two steel-jacketed bullets punched through the heavy metal tailgate. But no one was killed, and George, who took his foot off the accelerator just as a bullet came through it, was unhurt. Somehow he and the soldiers managed to get the truck back to Gulu.

The next day Jeffrey Latim, a brave Ugandan working with Habitat, went to the army garrison on his own and arranged for the truck to be released. He also talked the army brass into giving him an official letter forbidding soldiers to confiscate any trucks working on the Habitat project. Two days later the Habitat truck was hauling again.

In January of 1986, there was another coup in Uganda. We were quite concerned about Wil and Hulen Brown, our volunteers in Gulu. Our apprehension was heightened because some of the top officials of the deposed government were from Gulu, and we suspected they had fled back there. We didn't know what might happen. On February 1, however, we received a reassuring letter from Wil, a man of great faith and courage.

Hi Gang,

We're O.K.! Romans 8:35–39* and II Timothy 1:7† are the two Scriptures we hold to as we continue the work of God in Uganda. . . . Today our head carpenter and I made ten door frames and six window frames. The other workers have gone to their village in fear of the National Resistance Army coming to Gulu. We don't think that will happen. . . . Please call Hulen's dad and my mom and let them know we're okay!

Building houses for God's needy people, almost literally in the muzzle of a gun, is a pretty powerful statement of faith. It is also a shining example of peacemaking.

German Pomares, Nicaragua, is a rural community of approximately four hundred impoverished families. They live in small, vermin-infested palm thatch houses with earthen floors. In the midst of an ongoing political struggle, a handful of Habitat volunteers in Nicaragua built a kiln, put into operation a roof tile plant, set up a portable saw mill, stockpiled handmade soil-cement blocks, and began building houses. Even more important, the volunteers were building bridges of trust and encouragement between individuals. As one volunteer, Susan Bailey of Montclair, New Jersey, wrote: "People here have been beaten down so much, but through Habitat they are given the opportunity, resources, patience, and love to realize they can achieve a goal."

Another volunteer, Jim Hornsby, told us about his 6:30 A.M. daily Bible study and prayer time with the Habitat building crew.

Some are Sandinistas, most are not, but all love it and are hungry for Scripture. We've been able to share and pray with political leaders

---

* Who, then, can separate us from the love of Christ? Can trouble do it, or hardship or persecution or hunger or poverty or danger or death? As the scripture says, "For your sake we are in danger of death at all times; we are treated like sheep that are going to be slaughtered." No, in all things we have complete victory through him who loved us! For I am certain that nothing can separate us from his love: neither death nor life, neither angels nor other heavenly rulers or powers, neither the present nor the future, neither the world above nor the world below—there is nothing in all creation that will ever be able to separate us from the love of God which is ours through Christ Jesus our Lord.

† For the Spirit that God has given us does not make us timid; instead, his Spirit fills us with power, love and self-control.

and soldiers, Catholics and evangelicals, and farmers and teachers. The project itself is a witness. People know it is a demonstration of God's love. And it gives us an open door to share Christ. So we see not only house foundations being built, but Christian leadership as well.

On February 8, 1986, the Nicaragua project got a tremendous lift when it was visited by Jimmy and Rosalynn Carter, along with President Daniel Ortega and other government officials. Habitat homeowners demonstrated block and tile making and the portable saw mill. Presidents Carter and Ortega each laid a block, and together they mounted a doorway in the home of Enrique Torres.

Jimmy Carter said the Habitat project is "a visible demonstration of the love of Christ and the peace which comes with Christ."

Daniel Ortega responded that his government affirms "the freedom of religion, and putting Christian faith into working for justice and a better way of life." Foreign Minister Miguel D'Escoto, a Catholic priest, offered a prayer and President Ortega presented Bibles to the first two Habitat homeowners.

I hope and pray that our efforts in Nicaragua may help the cause of peace in that troubled land.

Sometimes we have been forced by local conditions to evacuate our volunteers temporarily. In 1981, Mennonite volunteers Lowell and Dianne Birkey of Manson, Iowa, were called home from Aguacatan, Guatemala, because mounting unrest there appeared too dangerous. Not until June of 1984 were new volunteers David and Becky Shiell of Fort Collins, Colorado, sent to Aguacatan. But despite a multitude of difficulties which slowed or sometimes stalled the building program, work continued. By 1986 more than a hundred families had moved from mostly cornstalk-and-mud huts to solid, earthquake-resistant homes, and new houses were going up at the rate of two to three per month. Our work in Guatemala, as elsewhere, is a serious effort to act out the biblical role of the peacemaker.

Habitat is building houses, and building community, all over the world, in unlikely places with unorthodox methods. The results are beautiful. Never forget that, if you get a crazy idea, and it comes from God, it will work.

A delightful illustration of this principle was told to me by Randle Dew of the Paducah, Kentucky, Habitat project. It seems that a used car dealer in the Paducah area took his dog, Spencer, everywhere with him, and featured him regularly on the dealership's television commercials. One day Randle decided to write a letter to Spencer to ask for a truck. The owner was intrigued. Within a short time, Paducah Habitat received two gifts: a used pickup truck and a challenge grant of a thousand dollars, which they quickly claimed by matching it with donated money.

Habitat folks even use a terminology that's different. "Vacation" is likely to mean taking time off from your regular job each year and traveling, at your own expense, to some distant project site, in order to spend that week or two laboring on a construction crew. For no pay. "Enough," in Habitat parlance, is not a great supply of anything; rather, it is whatever we have. We have learned that if we trust in God, He will take a few committed people and their seemingly small resources and multiply both to accomplish miracles. When it comes to housing developments, salesmen are likely to choose cute names like "Forest Glades" (even when there's not a tree in sight) or "Relaxing Acres." The Portland, Oregon, Habitat Committee, however, called their first three houses "Faith," "Hope," and "Love."

By way of explanation, the Portland group said that *faith* is what they purchased their first old house with in 1983; they *hoped* to find just the right family for the second renovated house nearby; and a new home was built right between the other two, with *love*. The third house, built by "vacationers" from several western states, was designed especially to meet the needs of a grandmother who was an amputee. She has now happily been enabled to rejoin her family.

On a personal note, Linda and I were touched by an idea our daughter Georgia had which her friends at school told her was crazy. In October of 1985 Georgia had wanted a special ring for her fourteenth birthday. At the same time, she was planning to go to New York City with us for Habitat's fall board meeting. She knew we had both worked hard during the two weeks at the Lower East Side tenement, and one day she announced unexpectedly, "I want you to give my birthday money to the New York Habitat project."

Proud dad that I was, when the offering was taken at the huge Habitation service in Grace Episcopal Church on October 11, 1985, I announced that Georgia was donating a fifty-dollar check in lieu of her birthday ring. Following the service, Julia McCray of Oakland, California, who had formerly spent a year in Americus as a volunteer, came up to me.

"I want to give this to Georgia," she said.

She held in her hand a beautiful gold ring in the shape of a dolphin, which had been a gift to her on her sixteenth birthday. Julia said she had enjoyed the ring for ten years and now wanted to pass it on. Georgia, who loves dolphins, was absolutely thrilled.

The next afternoon, as the entire Habitat gathering paraded across the Brooklyn Bridge to the dedication of the building on the Lower East Side, a Habitat supporter from Knoxville, Kay Benson, came up and handed me a handsome garnet ring.

"I want to give this to Georgia," she said.

Georgia was astonished, and very grateful.

About two weeks later I was in Atlanta with Andrew Young.

"When I was in Hong Kong last week," he told me, "I bought a ring for my daughter Paula, and another one for Georgia." He handed me an exquisite gold ring with a small jade stone.

I thanked him profusely, and then shared the story of what had been happening since Georgia gave her birthday money to New York City Habitat.

He chuckled appreciatively. "Well, you know," he reminded me, "the Bible tells us that when you give to the Lord you receive back a hundredfold. Be sure you get in touch with me when Georgia gets the other ninety-seven rings!"

I have no way of knowing how many more unexpected blessings, for her or for others, may have resulted from Georgia's gift. But

I do know this: Her school friends stopped ridiculing her crazy ideas.

Most of the people in the world simply do not understand how God's amazing promises operate. And to trust Him, to take Him at His word, is much too risky for them. Habitat folks know that trusting is the *only* way. It works.

11

A Technology That's Appropriate

Habitat volunteers have to be versatile. They must be ready to stretch every talent they possess and to develop some new ones at the same time. Particularly when they work overseas among different languages and cultures, volunteers learn that unexpected challenges are part of every day's work.

In November 1979 Pat Clark, of Salem County, New Jersey, went to Ntondo, Zaire, to work in community development. Earlier that year Pat had completed her studies at Smith College with a major in government and economics. During her first few months in Ntondo, Pat worked with the local carpenters, making doors, windows, and trusses for Habitat houses. Later, when another volunteer was ill, Pat moved temporarily to Mbandaka, Zaire, to head up the project there, and this dynamic young black woman found herself supervising a work force of some thirty-five men. Neither of these jobs had been the focus of any of her college courses.

Returning to Ntondo, Pat found that the women of the village wanted her to organize literacy classes. Few women there could read or write. Working in the fields from 6:00 A.M. to 4:00 P.M., in addition to shouldering family responsibilities, left little time for other pursuits. Yet the classes grew, and soon sessions in French, English, and nutrition were also being offered. Then Pat, who had never been a seamstress, started a sewing class in her little house which eventually drew one hundred women. They even opened a small store to finance their projects. But by this time, the gatherings had outgrown every available meeting place in Ntondo.

Pat and a local committee of twelve women—two from each section of the village—held a consultation. They needed a building specifically designed for their own programs. In order to make this construction possible, the women decided to undertake a formidable task: *they would produce all the forty thousand bricks themselves.*

The fired bricks which Pat introduced in Ntondo would be made from local mud and baked in a stack called a clamp, five thousand at a time. She discovered, however, that the initial enthusiasm evidenced by the women at their big planning meeting dwindled when it was time actually to get involved. They already had heavy work schedules, and besides, women did the farming, and construction jobs were traditionally reserved for men.

So every morning for the first two weeks, Pat went alone to the work site to "throw" bricks. When she returned to her other chores, another row of neatly molded rectangles was drying in the sun.

One morning a member of the women's committee stopped beside Pat, astounded. "You're really serious about making these bricks!"

At that point the first bystander became a brickmaker. Within a few days several other women were coming on a regular basis. Then the women's committee decided that anyone who did not help make bricks would be excluded from the popular afternoon classes. From that time on the brickmakers were out each day in force.

Throwing bricks is hard work, but there was fun on the job as well. Children played constantly around the perimeter of the project—mud pies are universal toys—and mothers took breaks to nurse babies and share local news. A steady stream of men from the village came out to watch, hoping to find support for their firm conviction that women are simply not capable of making bricks.

One man was particularly impressed. After observing the work on several occasions, he expressed his reaction to Pat: "We know you care, because you are out working *with* us. The Belgians never worked with us like this."

On April 25, 1982 a huge celebration in Ntondo marked the dedication of the women's center. Visitors came by plane, truck, dugout canoe, and by foot. Some traveled from as far away as the capital city of Kinshasa, a distance of three hundred and thirty miles. The four-hour ceremony featured impassioned speeches and presentations along with joyous singing and dancing. Pat still savors one special surprise she had planned. Each of the twelve members of her local committee left the service proudly holding a new T-Shirt. On the front, the Habitat logo was displayed; on the back were the carefully stencilled Lingala words "Basi na Tondo" (Women of Ntondo).

The completed women's center includes an area for health and nutrition studies, a classroom, a store, and a spacious general purpose room for sewing classes and other meetings. On special occasions when a large assembly hall is required, it is used by all the villagers.

Pat's efforts in brickmaking with local materials are just one example of an important and relatively new approach to physical and social development in the third world. This emphasis is usually referred to as "appropriate technology."

Instead of the capital-intensive, labor-saving technologies we are accustomed to developing in the Western world, Habitat makes a conscious effort to employ the reverse: methods which are labor-intensive and capital-saving. This often means returning to techniques of earlier generations, sometimes enhancing them with the knowledge of the late twentieth century. It also means utilizing as fully as possible both human and natural resources which are available in the area, as Pat Clark was able to do in Ntondo.

In many countries where Habitat is working, the inflation rate is incredible. It was 300 percent in Guatemala in 1985. In Bolivia, one dollar was worth twenty pesos in 1980; by June of 1985, one dollar was worth *three hundred thousand* pesos! The only possible way to build housing which is affordable for the poor in such economies is to employ as much as possible local materials like clay and wood, which are not tied to the inflation factor.

A good example of appropriate technology in housing is the hand-operated CINVA-Ram block press. Developed in Colombia in the late 1950s, it has been used extensively throughout the third world to make rammed earth building blocks. The long handle on the CINVA-Ram press allows a blockmaker to apply great pressure to the soil mixture, thereby improving the quality of the product. Still more durable blocks can be turned out with the addition of small amounts of cement to the mix.

In our first overseas Habitat project, in Mbandaka, Zaire, we rehabilitated an old, worn out but labor-intensive electric block-making machine. It became the basis for launching that project. Years later that block machine was still functioning and still turning out thousands of sturdy building blocks, steadily increasing the number of houses for the poor in that capital city of the equator region. At the same time, the machine was providing jobs in an area where unemployment and underemployment are in the neighborhood of 70 percent. CINVA-Ram block machines have gradually been introduced in the other Zaire projects, and they have been readily accepted by local residents.

When the Habitat project in Guatemala was launched in 1979 by volunteer Bob Stevens (Bob later became our director of all overseas operations), the CETA-ram block press was employed. This machine was a Guatemalan modification of the CINVA-Ram.

Yet another refinement in block making appeared after Harry Sangree, a Dartmouth engineering student, read *Bokotola* in 1979 and decided to become a Habitat volunteer in Zaire. Harry returned home and spent several years developing the DART-Ram, an efficient labor-intensive machine which can produce more blocks per hour than similar presses. With the aid of a small grant from Habitat and additional assistance from several churches, Harry was able to complete modifications on his machine. It has been field tested in our overseas projects, and in 1983 U.S. Patent 4,406,606 was awarded for "an apparatus for producing soil building blocks."

Construction in the early Habitat programs centered around the use of cement. Although cement is probably the most widespread "modern" building material, its production and transportation are based upon petroleum. If alternatives can be found, depending less upon cement, the cost of houses can generally be further reduced.

To that end, Habitat has begun in several locations to try to relearn the production techniques of making simple clay bricks for firing in small, wood-burning kilns. This requires the availability of both good clay and firewood. In addition, Habitat volunteers are studying the possibilities of using rammed earth for walls in areas where firewood is difficult or expensive to obtain. Properly constructed, on a sound foundation, and properly shielded from the rain, such walls can last several hundred years!

Habitat is also looking for viable alternatives to the corrugated iron roof, used almost universally in developing countries. (Referred to as a "tin" roof, this material usually contains no tin.) Except for thatch—which is a serious fire hazard and which harbors insects, rodents, and snakes—corrugated iron is the most common and most preferred roof in the third world.

Westerners are not likely to be thrilled with a metal roof in the tropics. The heat is stifling on sunny days, and on rainy days the noise is deafening. Among low-income families in developing countries, however, it is seen as the ideal roof: It is lightweight, long lasting, easy to build, and "permanent."

Unfortunately, in recent years that so-called permanence has become more and more brief. As skyrocketing inflation shoots the cost of raw materials and transportation practically out of sight, the gauge used in iron roofing has been steadily reduced. In very humid zones, rust may now appear on the new roof within three or four years, and as a result it probably will not last the life of a twenty-year Habitat mortgage.

Furthermore, a metal roof makes third world people dependent on imported Western manufactured materials. And because of transportation and import charges, this roof may represent 50 percent of the cost of a simple house. If you walk about an African city today, you will see hundreds of houses with the walls up but no roofs—and they often stay that way for years. An impoverished citizen can scrimp and save and manage to buy a few cement blocks at a time until finally he has enough to build the walls of a house. But then he can never get enough money together all at once to put on the roof!

A variety of possibilities has been studied in recent years for alternative roofing materials—cement, natural fibers (sisal, hemp, or jute) with sulfur, asphalt-impregnated wood fiber, hardwood shingles, and improved thatch, to name a few. In Nicaragua, the Habitat project has enlisted the aid of an oldtimer in the area to teach a younger generation his skill in making Spanish tile roofs from local clay. In Haiti, volunteers have constructed arches of ferrocement (a rich mixture of cement over chicken wire), offering a new and inexpensive dome-shaped roof.

As Habitat struggles to make simple, decent houses affordable for the world's needy people, however, we must avoid two important areas of *inappropriate* technology.

First, without local involvement and leadership, innovations will not be accepted. In every country in the world, poor families aspire to a house that looks modern and affluent. If a specific material or design appears to be old-fashioned or is identified with poverty, it will be unacceptable to a person of any income level.

Habitat for Humanity's approach to housing is much more than just the application of appropriate technology. A vital concept we employ is partnership, not patronage. Our volunteers seek to build relationships along with houses, introducing alternative building methods as they become available, but leaving the final decision on the type of construction to the local citizens. To attempt to dictate which technology an area should adopt would be paternalistic, or simply another form of colonialism.

Some years ago I spoke on Habitat in a Presbyterian Church in Atlanta, Georgia. Traveling with me was Sam Mompongo, project director in his village of Ntondo, Zaire. Sam, a graduate of Washington State University, is one of those rare citizens among developing countries who, after traveling abroad and obtaining a first-class education, returned home for the express purpose of helping his people.

On the day we visited the church in Atlanta, a number of architecture students from Georgia Tech came over to hear about the housing projects we had started in Africa. When Sam and I had both shared some of our experiences, the floor was opened for questions. One of the students stood up.

"Why are you putting tin roofs on the houses you build? Indigenous materials like grass or palm branches should be used in tropical countries."

"People in Zaire prefer tin," Sam answered simply.

"But tin is certainly not native to your culture."

"I have observed in the United States," Sam replied mildly, "that you have appropriated ideas and materials that you like from other countries. You have Greek architecture and Japanese cars— and pizza! There is carpet on this floor. Carpet is a good idea for Atlanta, but in the tropics carpet makes no sense. However, tin roofs make a lot of sense to people in Zaire, because sometimes it rains every day there, and people want a roof that doesn't leak."

No matter how many explanations Sam offered, the young man remained unmoved. It was awful, he insisted, that an imported material was being used to house the people of Zaire.

After a few more questions the session ended, and was followed by a time of refreshments. As people stood around chatting, Sam suddenly hurried over to me. With a knowing smile, he announced, "I just found out why that young man did not want us to have tin roofs. He's from France. He's a *colonialist!*"

The second area of technological inappropriateness to be avoided is experimentation. In a process of trial and error, some efforts will inevitably fail; poor families cannot afford this. Habitat folks are adamant on this point: We will not experiment on the poor.

Frequently people describe to us a new technique, suggesting that we try it out in India, or Papua New Guinea, where we are building for dirt-poor families the first decent living conditions they have ever known. Our reply is always the same: We will be glad to learn more about these methods *after* they have been thoroughly tested. Most professional schools train people to serve the affluent.[1] Our purpose is to serve the needy. To that end, we try to find the best technologies that others have developed and apply them wherever they are workable and culturally acceptable.[2]

In Zaire, volunteer LuAnn Goodall successfully introduced the Lorena stove, an idea that had originally been developed by CIDA, a Canadian agency, in Guatemala. [The stove's name comes from the Spanish *lodo* (mud) and *arena* (sand) with the two words carefully combined, since no one wants a "mud stove"!] Built out of adobe blocks, the stoves are individually constructed with holes on the top to fit each woman's cooking pots. About 40 percent less wood is required for the Lorena stove than for an open fire. And these stoves measurably reduce the hazard of respiratory diseases like tuberculosis because women are no longer forced to breathe smoke for several hours every day.

In Haiti, the use of a poured concrete wall has dramatically lowered building costs. An "old style" concrete block Habitat house cost $1692 in 1984; changing to the poured wall resulted in a total cost of $1360. In addition, more labor on these houses can now be done by unskilled family members, and the important aspect of partnership and involvement has been strengthened.

Habitat is always investigating fresh approaches to standard building methods. We want to find better ways to construct earthquake- and hurricane-resistant structures without increasing costs. We are working on various designs for composting latrines. We are constructing in Americus several full-size demonstration houses, of various types used in developing countries, to give volunteers more hands-on experience before they go overseas. And in the works is a paperback Basic Construction Reference Manual, a simple textbook to be used by non-experts *with* non-experts, in which Habitat will tie together ideas and expertise in feasible technology gathered from all over the world.

Obviously, no single technology will be feasible in all areas. But every one, if it is to be appropriate at all, should be:

1) Understood and accepted by the community;

2) Developed and employed with the active involvement of local people;

3) Low in capital cost in that location;

4) Designed to utilize locally available materials as much as possible;

5) Capable of providing jobs within the local economy;

6) Usable even in remote villages;

7) Uncomplicated enough that people without a high level of formal education can maintain it;

8) Structured so that local workers can adapt the technique to changing circumstances; and

9) Free from regulation by royalties, patents, duties, or other fees.

That's a big order. But if we are even to approach our stupendous goal of eliminating poverty housing from the earth, we must investigate every idea that just might bring that goal closer. We will continue to do this.

One Habitat for Humanity building technique, however, will never change. Whatever kind of mortar goes into the joints, there will always be *love* in it.

---

1   There are some notable exceptions, among them: Drexel University, Philadelphia, Pennsylvania, Curriculum in Appropriate Technology; Eastern College, St. David's, Pennsylvania, MBA in Economic Development; School for International Training, Brattleboro, Vermont, Certificate of Advance Studies in International Development; Warren Wilson College, Asheville, North Carolina, International Development Program; and Western University, Cullowhee, North Carolina, Center for Improving Mountain Living.

2   The following organizations are some that are developing technologies that are appropriate for the poor: A.T. International, Washington, D.C.; Creative Ministries, Columbia, Missouri; S.C.A.T. (Swiss Center for Appropriate Technology), St. Gallen, Switzerland; N.C.A.T. (National Center for Appropriate Technology), Butte, Montana; Asian Institute of Technology, Bangkok, Thailand; S.I.F.A.T. (Southern Institute for Appropriate Technology), Wedowee, Alabama; I.T.D.G. (Intermediate Technology Development Group), West Midlands, England.

12

A Day of Prayer and Action

The prayer of a good person has a powerful effect."* Habitat folks believe that. Statements like "the Father will give you whatever you ask of him in my name"† and "if you believe, you will receive whatever you ask for in prayer"‡ are cornerstones in the foundation of faith on which Habitat is built.

We begin every working day in Americus with a time of devotions and prayer shared by volunteers, visitors, and staff at the Habitat office. A similar practice is followed at Habitat projects the world over. Again and again, we experience the manifold blessings of prayer which the Scriptures promise.

In his Christmas 1985 letter from Appalachia Habitat in Tennessee, Project Director Jim Billington told us about some of the challenges the past twelve months had brought to the group there.

* James 5:16
† John 15:16
‡ Matthew 2:22

And he related how they had met these challenges.

> In March of this year, we were very worried. We had a list of housing applications as long as a country road, and a list of unpaid bills even longer!
>
> At our next Board meeting, we agreed to pray, *every morning*, for the Lord to take hold of our work and transform it into a work of praise to Him.
>
> Everything began to change. Two hundred volunteers came to Robbins over the summer, each bringing a different and unique skill. We asked for funds, over and over again, and funds began to come. We asked for expertise in building skills, and the right person always seemed to pop up at the right time.
>
> In early August, we were doing foundation work on the log home we had started. By this time our construction supervisor had gone, and we were left with only us amateur, long-term volunteers to do the job. But then a group from Chattanooga showed up, and sure enough—one of its members, Bob McElheney, does this stuff for a living!
>
> With the power of the Lord, all things *can* be made new again!

Amen, Jim. And without the power of the Lord, we won't accomplish much. Our efforts will flounder unless they are undergirded by regular, faithful, *believing* prayer.

Habitat folks also believe in action. After we have prayed, turning our needs, our problems, and our frustrations over to the Lord, and thanking Him for the help that we know will come, then we get busy. After all, that's the same procedure Jesus followed when He had just two fish and five loaves of bread to feed five thousand people. And the results were pretty amazing.

At the spring Habitat board meeting in 1981 held in the First United Methodist Church in Fort Myers, Florida, a group of half a dozen Habitat advisors shared a brainstorming session. They were seeking ways that Habitat's rapidly enlarging ministry could continue to keep in close touch with the Power at the center. At the same time, they wanted to involve more concerned people in prayer support for the projects.

Out of this small meeting, a great idea emerged. There should be one day designated each year when people everywhere would pray in a special, concentrated way about the worldwide need for decent housing.

The recommendation, however, as it was finally drafted for a subsequent board meeting, was not just to pray. All of us were aware of the World Day of Prayer, observed each year on the first Friday in March. We affirmed that observance, and the idea behind it. At the same time, we felt a need for a separate day of prayer focused entirely on the desperate problem of inadequate shelter. But still more than that was called for. A favorite Habitat Bible verse says, "Our love should not be just words and talk; it must be true love, which shows itself in action."*

We wanted a day of prayer *and action.*

Over the next year, Habitat people continued to discuss ways to implement this powerful idea. I corresponded extensively about it with Dolores Van Loucks, of Los Gatos, California, coordinator for the advisors. At the fall board meeting in Americus in 1982, we took the first step. We decided to seek a million names on a petition to create an International Day of Prayer and Action for Human Habitat, to be observed on the third Sunday of September every year. Our Seventh Anniversary Celebration was planned for the following fall in Indianapolis, and the meeting would close on the third Sunday in September. We would present our petitions to church leaders at that celebration, encouraging them to promote the idea. At the same time, on that weekend we would observe our first International Day of Prayer and Action for Human Habitat.

Along with the November 1982 issue of our Habitat newsletter, the following petition was enclosed.

We, the undersigned, do humbly and urgently call upon people of good will, especially people of faith and all churches, to observe the third Sunday of September hereafter as

INTERNATIONAL DAY OF PRAYER AND ACTION FOR HUMAN HABITAT

This call is motivated by our deep concern for the countless millions of people who do not have a simple, decent place in which to live.

* 1 John 3:18

God calls us to be personally involved in solving this great social problem in our world. We believe that we should not live contentedly in adequate homes, giving lip service only to the command of Jesus to love our neighbor as we love ourselves.

We are committed to prayer and action to solve this worldwide problem of inadequate housing, and we call upon YOU to join us.

Each petition sheet had a place for name, city, state, and country for twenty people. We were making a grassroots attempt to create worldwide awareness of the pitiful living conditions of so many people. It was at once consciousness-raising and a call to action.

The Habitat newsletter urged our supporters to circulate these petitions in their churches. We encouraged readers to make additional copies or to write to the Habitat office for more petitions. We advised that signers were to be told that their names would not be put on any mailing lists. Indeed, we did not even ask for street addresses. They could contribute to Habitat—we were working to raise an extra million dollars in connection with our Seventh Anniversary Celebration—but that was not necessary. The important thing was to increase sensitivity, as people became committed to pray and to become involved in some way in solving the problem of inadequate shelter. They could act through Habitat for Humanity, or privately, or through their church or some other group. We simply wanted people to pray and then to *do something.*

We were able to get many Christian leaders to sign the petition; they in turn recruited others to join in this movement. Hundreds of Habitat supporters set about gathering signatures and enlisting involvement through their local churches. In the United States, Canada, and Europe, we secured thousands of names, but the pacesetter in the campaign was the Peru Habitat organization. Under Zenon Colque Rojas' aggressive leadership, they had amassed more than twenty thousand signatures by the time of our Indianapolis Celebration in September 1983.

In some places overseas, the petitions presented problems. In Haiti, for example, there was so much suspicion about practically everything that people were simply afraid to sign. As a result, we obtained few signatures from there. In the African projects there were always logistical difficulties, first in getting petitions copied and circulated, and later in retrieving them and transporting them back to Georgia.

That September, one of the highlights of our Seventh Anniversary Celebration was Dolores Van Loucks' presentation of the petitions to an array of leaders from several denominations. We had obtained a total of sixty thousand names, and they were recorded in a stack of paper that rose two feet high on the platform. At the very least, we had managed to make sixty thousand people think seriously about a problem that has too long been largely ignored. And we determined to continue reaching for our goal of a million signatures.

In order to boost the Day of Prayer and Action from another direction, we began offering church bulletin inserts to be used each third Sunday in September. Every year the use of these inserts increases. Over three hundred and fifty thousand were ordered in 1985. They include a brief explanation of the worldwide housing need on one side, and a litany to be read by pastor and congregation on the other. In 1984 the bulletin insert included the litany below.

LITANY FOR HUMAN HABITAT

Leader: The Lord Jesus is homeless!

People: Homeless! When was that?

Leader: When he was a little boy standing at the edge of that garbage dump in Guatemala. Remember? You saw him on your TV, the one you have in your den. You also saw him when he was an old man sitting on the porch of his rented shack in South Georgia. You noticed him as you drove by in your new air-conditioned car, on the way to your vacation home.

People: That little boy and that old man—they were Jesus?

Leader: Yes. And you have seen him also in the slums of Haiti. Remember those dreadful pictures of poverty housing and those sad-looking people you saw in that magazine? You have seen him, too, in India, in Africa, in the inner cities of New York and Chicago, and even in your home town.

People: What do you expect us to do about it?

Leader: First of all, realize in your hearts that all of those hurting, homeless people are the Lord, in distressing disguise. Then, pray and act to find solutions to the problem.

People: But the problem is so big, and we are so few and small.

Leader: If the Lord is for you, who can be against you? Faith the size of a mustard seed can move mountains and rebuild cities. If five loaves and two fish could feed five thousand, surely the bricks and boards we have can house millions.

People: First we'll build a few more sanctuaries for worshipping, and a few more universities to study the problem.

Leader: Worship God in spirit and in truth! Pews are empty, but tenements are overflowing. Studies have already been made; now people need to put faith into action. Worship services must lead to worshipful service.

People: In our worship, we will pray for an end to substandard housing in the world. In our service, we will seek to put Christ's love into action, knowing that prayers are answered through us as we give and step out in faith.

All: Lord God, you have given us a place to live, people to live with, and a world to build in. Open our eyes to the needs of others. Make us concerned enough to help and comfort them so that your love may be seen in this world, through Jesus Christ our Lord. Amen.

Each September, on the International Day of Prayer and Action for Human Habitat, pastors are urged to preach sermons about worldwide needs in housing. Special offerings can be taken for the work of Habitat for Humanity, or for other groups that are working to bring about better housing conditions. If not the entire service, at least a "moment for mission" can be devoted, on that Sunday, to the problem of poverty housing.

We have been gratified by reports of the ways that people around the world have chosen to observe that day, with prayer and also with action.

In Pickens, South Carolina, the Habitat group dedicated a new house.

The Church at Woodmoor, in Monument, Colorado, presented a Habitat representative with a gift of fifteen hundred dollars to build a house in Haiti.

The Parkway United Church of Christ in Town and Country, Missouri, welcomed home two Habitat volunteer builders from their congregation, and offered church support for others who may decide to go.

New Covenant Congregational Church in Hampton, New Hampshire, voted to build a Habitat house in India.

First Baptist Church in Madison, Wisconsin, heard an inspiring sermon on shelter. Habitat Advisor Sterling Schallert, a member of that congregation, proposed that the church build a house in Haiti, and they responded by building one in Haiti and another in Bolivia!

First Baptist Church in Melrose, Massachusetts, where Habitat President David Rowe serves as pastor, observed a "blessing of homes" that Sunday afternoon. At the invitation of church members, David visited in several homes. A time of fellowship included a prayer of thanksgiving at each house, reminding parishioners of the blessing of good housing, and enlarging their concern for others who are not similarly blessed.

John and Mary Pritchard, directors of the Kansas City Habitat project, spoke to two churches about Habitat that morning and spent the rest of the day hiking. Since they had fasted the entire day, they sent a check for the cost of their meals to Habitat.

Mason Schumacher of Habitat's Rocky Mountain Regional Center in Boulder, Colorado, even went to jail on the Day of Prayer and Action in 1985! He spoke to inmates about Habitat, asking them to pray for decent shelter around the world, and to think about how they could help after they were released.

The United Church of Cloverdale, California, a congregation of less than one hundred members, raised over three thousand dollars for the Santa Rosa Habitat project. Parishioner Helen Campbell also sent us signed petition forms and a long list of names to be added to the Habitat mailing list.

A small Missionary Baptist parish in Harlem Heights, a low-income neighborhood on the edge of Fort Myers, Florida, received a special offering for the local Habitat project. It came to $360.16.

Clyde and Nancy Tilley invited Tom Hall, from the Americus office, to speak at four churches in Jackson, Tennessee, and to meet with local people interested in starting a Habitat project.

Thanks to many persuasive Habitat supporters, in September 1985 the governors of eleven states issued proclamations concerning the Day of Prayer and Action and Habitat for Humanity Week (Colorado, Connecticut, Georgia, Illinois, Indiana, Kansas, Louisiana, New York, South Carolina, Utah, and Wisconsin).

We have also learned about a variety of exciting observances of the Day of Prayer and Action by Habitat projects overseas.

In Puno, Peru, preparations for the 1984 Day of Prayer and Action had gone on for six months. Getting ready for this occasion consisted of carving a ditch, using picks and shovels, two and a half kilometers uphill through volcanic rock! When the Habitat workers finally reached their destination, a spring of fresh water, they laid a pipeline in the ditch. At the close of a special service on the Day of Prayer and Action, the pipeline was opened. Immediately, precious water began to flow to a just-completed water tank equipped with two faucets convenient to the new Habitat homes. Later, as individual families could afford it, pipes would be purchased and a small fee charged for their hook-up. But never again would water have to be hand-carried from a stream over a mile away. Homeowners, volunteers, and visitors shared this day in a celebration of joy.

Sarah Hornsby, of Cullowhee, North Carolina, a Habitat volunteer in Nicaragua, wrote us in the fall of 1985 about their project's observance of this special day.

The International Day of Prayer and Action for Human Habitat was a first for us in Nicaragua. We invited the evangelical pastors and congregations to attend with their musicians, along with nuns from El Viejo, joining the Catholic majority here. We held the meeting in the open air pavilion, "The Palacial." One hundred and fifty people attended. Now we plan to have this type of worship service the first Sunday of every month, binding the community together in love.

The children had practiced their folk dancing all week at our house. Marguerita, the teacher, asked me for paper to make flags—blue and white for Nicaragua, red and black for Sandinista, and red, white and blue for the United States flag. I even found some silver stars.

Then we made flags for the countries that have Habitat projects. The children carried the flags, singing a song that names each of the countries in the Americas: "America is for Christ." Three guitars, Jim's bass made out of a barrel, maracas, and a banjo made lively music!

We prayed for Habitat projects all over the world. We ask you to pray for us, too, as we plan expansion of Habitat Nicaragua.

In Gulu, Uganda, Arthur E. Oryem, secretary of the local Habitat for Humanity committee, reported they met regularly "to draw up a suitable program" for the 1984 Day of Prayer and Action. The resulting observance was thoroughly ecumenical, and exhibited a beautiful blend of prayer and action.

The functions took place at Laliya Habitat Estates project site. The members of the Executive Committee, Habitat house-occupants, potential house-occupants, students from Archbishop Janani Luwum Theological College, and others assembled at the site at about 10:30 in the morning. They had brought with them their packed lunches.

Groundbreaking for a house foundation started soon after the assembling. Some people went to load stones onto the Habitat dump truck; others crushed stones on a building foundation with a heavy hammer; a few went to fetch drinking water for the congregation. After work, everyone sat down to eat lunch. Different dishes were exchanged among the people, indicating true love and mutual understanding.

At the end of lunch, there was an open-air service which was conducted by Vicar Monsignor Celestine A. A. Odong (Catholic) and Rev. Charles Okech (Protestant). In their sermons, the two clergymen emphasized ideal Christian life, cooperation, love and good will. The Theological College students (Habitat Tabernacle Choir) sang during and after the service. They also translated the litany into the language of the people. Speeches on Habitat philosophy and the Habitat movement were given by the Executive Committee Vice-Chairman, the Directors, and the Secretary.

Then there was the photographing of the potential Habitat house-occupants in front of their houses or on their allocated plots. One could see smiling faces everywhere!

The congregation departed for home about 5:30 in the evening. It was indeed a true day of prayer and action.

The Dumay, Haiti, project, begun in 1982 in an area of desperate poverty, has faithfully participated in the Day of Prayer and Action. In 1985 volunteer Pam Hanson of Houston, Texas, who was working in the Haiti project along with her husband, Carl, and their infant son, Ian, wrote a letter home about their day. She included an important observation.

"For us here in Dumay," Pam said, "I think it is especially significant that we had so many churches praying. That's one thing everyone can do, no matter how poor they are!"

Our fervent hope is that before long the International Day of Prayer and Action for Human Habitat will be regularly observed by millions of people in every country on earth. That's something everyone can do, no matter how rich or poor they are. And if they are indeed rich, they can do a lot more.

Most of us in Western nations are truly wealthy in comparison with the rest of the world. Habitat invites everyone, rich and poor alike, to join us in prayer on the third Sunday of every September.

And then we invite you to join us in action.

Above: Volunteers Greg and Barbara Garrett *(left)* and Karen Foreman *(right)* with the local Habitat committee in Gemena, Zaire.

Below: Millard celebrates with new homeowners in Peru.

Becky Sheill uses a CETA-Ram in Guatemala *(left)* and Julie Knop demonstrates a CINVA-Ram in Nicaragua *(right)* used to make bricks from local materials.

Above: Workers dry home-made clay tiles for roofs in Nicaragua. Right: Jim Hornsby uses a portable sawmill at a Nicaraguan project site.

Above: Most families in Dumay, Haiti, live in shacks like this one.

Right: Cheerful local workers in Gulu, Uganda.

Left: Mixing mud to make bricks in Kenya.

Right: A local mason lays h·o·m·e·m·a·d·e bricks for Habitat housing in Gulu, Uganda. (Photo by Bill Moore.)

Left: The walls of row houses go up quickly in Puno, Peru.

...ht: Prayer circle ...ncluding a ...use blessing ...emony in San ...onio, Texas.

Left: A proud family stands on the porch of their newly reha- bilitated house in Pickens County, South Carolina.

13

God's Incidents

often meet with groups who are considering the formation of a new Habitat for Humanity project. One of the most frequently asked questions is, "How much money do we need to raise before we begin?"

My answer is always the same: "A dollar. If you have less than a dollar, launching a project would be irresponsible."

Then I explain that there is one other requirement.

"You must also have a core group of committed people who are serious about serving the Lord using the economics of Jesus, and about helping His children find a decent place to live. If you have the dollar and the committed people, and you move on faith, the Lord will move with you."

In fact, as Steve Anderson, of Chesapeake Habitat in Baltimore, frequently reminds us, "When you step out in faith and let the Lord lead, you have to *run* to keep up!"

As the ministry of Habitat grows, amazing things keep happening to help the work along. When *Love in the Mortar Joints* was published in 1980, a chapter full of these episodes was included, titled "God's Coincidences."

Similar stories poured in during 1985 as we were gathering material for this book. Among the comments we received was an interesting one from Tom McLaughlin, a Catholic layman who heads Coastal Empire Habitat in Savannah, Georgia.

"I hate to start off a letter on a disagreeing note," he wrote, "but I have to take issue with your 'God's Coincidences.' We don't see them that way. God is working *with* us, taking a direct hand in what we are doing!"

You're right, of course, Tom. So this time I'll share some examples of the ways His hand has clearly been involved in helping us, and frankly call them "God's Incidents."

I'll begin with one of Tom's own experiences. It took place, Tom told us, during the early stages of the Savannah project.

> The hole for the footings for our first house had been dug. The steel rebar was in place, and Lou Castilion and I were waiting for the other volunteers and the concrete truck to arrive. At 3:30 P.M. the truck arrived, but no volunteers. Lou and I, both age sixty-five, took a deep breath and started spreading the concrete in the hole. As we were beginning our struggles, a young man came up and told us he was looking for work. Lou told him we were doing God's work, and that we were building this house for a poor family, using free labor. He pondered Lou's words for a few minutes. Then he peeled off his jacket, turned to the truck driver and said, "Let's go to work." As he took the hoe from me he said, "I've been doing this kind of thing for eight years." He worked the concrete into place efficiently, picked up his jacket and went on his way.
>
> We had never seen the young man before, and we haven't seen him since. We don't remember his name, but we know God sent him. We thanked God for His helping hand, and for the grace to recognize it.

When the Denver, Colorado, Habitat project was getting started, they were donated a house, on condition that it be relocated to a vacant lot purchased by Habitat. The house could not be moved, however, until another construction project, planned for the house site, received approval. There were frustrating delays. Finally the project was approved, and the donors phoned to inform Habitat that the house had to be moved within two weeks.

With some trepidation, a call was made immediately to the house mover. He had been contacted earlier, and had told Denver Habitat to give him plenty of advance notice. After checking his schedule, he announced that the following week was the only available time he had for the next three months!

The house was moved first to a lot which had been vacant for years, just across an alley behind the Habitat parcel. The neighboring lot was ideally located so that the house could be lined up on it and then pulled onto the Habitat site in perfect position. There was no other possible access route to the Habitat lot.

The next morning, the mover got a call from the owner of the vacant land.

"Move that house immediately," the caller said. "We are going to start building on that ground!"

The donated house was promptly shifted to its proper place on the Habitat lot, and, like Moses and the Red Sea, the vacant space closed in behind them.

One of the sparkplugs of Habitat for Humanity Mid-South, headquartered in Memphis, is a determined lady named Fran Collier. She recounted, in a letter to me, a whole series of discouragements which the group confronted as they tried to find land in Rossville, Tennessee, an area where poverty housing was abysmal. Then, wrote Fran, God's amazing incidents began to happen, and a lot and the money to buy it both appeared at the same time. From there on, the incidents just kept coming.

> The land was purchased and construction got under way. Our first house was designated for Anna Spencer and her family: five sons, a daughter, and three grandchildren. The shack they lived in was unbelievable. There were three rooms for ten people. There was no running water, no well, not even an outhouse. The "facilities" were the bushes. The low ceilings and walls were lined with flattened cardboard boxes in a vain effort to keep out cold winter air. Electricity consisted of stray wires and a few exposed light bulbs. The floor

was so rickety that even a small child running across it made the house shake.

To replace this miserable shack, Habitat planned a sturdy four-bedroom, one bath, concrete-block house of just more than a thousand square feet. The Spencers were thrilled, and they were anxious to help in every way they could, to speed up the work. However, neither they nor any of our other Habitat volunteers knew how to lay blocks. Concrete blocks for the house had been donated, but who would lay them?

"You'll have to get some skilled blocklayers," everyone said.

"But where?"

"Try the Bricklayers' Union."

When I called the union president, he allowed as how they wouldn't mind my coming to their meeting to try to get volunteers, but he didn't hold out much hope for success.

As the men filed into the meeting hall, I got very strange looks indeed. Then, when I asked them to work on Saturdays—their day off—for no pay (they make fourteen dollars an hour), it was clear they thought I was crazy. When I said they would be helping to build a decent house for some of God's people in need, a house which would be sold with a no-profit, no-interest mortgage, all doubt was removed. They *knew* I was crazy! But later, when I passed around the sign-up sheet, three men signed. That was all we needed. Thanks be to God!

On January 3, 1985, the Spencers moved into their beautiful new home, and we dedicated it on February 16. Friends, family members and Habitat partners gathered joyfully in their front yard to help them celebrate this great event. The dedication service prompted an excellent article in our local newspaper, and that precipitated another of the Lord's miracles.

A concerned Christian gentleman called me. He introduced himself as Jimmy Foster of Foster Auto World and asked a lot of questions about Habitat. When he finally paused for breath, I asked if he would by any chance have a pickup truck at Foster Auto World that he might be willing to give to Habitat. He said that pickup trucks are very expensive, and I assured him we'd be delighted to have a *used* one. He told me to call him back next week. I did. His first statement made me lose hope: "I've changed my mind about giving Habitat a used pickup truck." Then he added, "I'm going to give you a *new* truck!"

The rest of the story is typical of how giving creates giving. He said he was going to send his teenage son, who had had little exposure to people in need, to work with Habitat to build houses. And another man read about the donation in the paper and said, "If he can give a pickup truck, I can give my time," so we received still another talented volunteer!

Time and again, the Habitat people of Pickens County, South Carolina, have seen the Lord's hand in their work. Sandra Graham, one of the founders of that on-the-move group, shared one such occasion:

> From the time we started Viola Allen's house, we always seemed to be out of money. Yet each month we somehow paid the bills. As we neared completion, Roger Gettys called to tell me he had found a volunteer to install the floor covering, but of course there was no money for the covering. Roger and I agreed that we should take advantage of the volunteer, purchase the floor covering and hope the money came in to pay for it. The same day the bill came, a note from Father Bill Brimley, priest at St. Andrew's in Clemson, arrived. It said simply, "I asked my congregation to make a special offering for Habitat. I hope this will help." The check was for $600. The bill for the floor covering was exactly $592. The Lord supplied a little extra for carpet tacks!

In December 1984, a group of people met in Nashville, Tennessee, to discuss the possibility of forming a Habitat project. A unanimous decision was made to move ahead. At the same time, another local agency, Neighborhood Housing Service, was holding a board of directors meeting at which they decided to terminate their housing efforts in Nashville. As time passed, NHS came to see Habitat as its means of continuing a ministry in housing. They offered Habitat assistance, office supplies, desks—and ten vacant lots!

When the new group needed a board of directors, the positions and people came almost automatically. The director of NHS became one of the Habitat directors. A big need, however, was someone to serve as chairman of the building committee. The day of the nominations and elections, Bill Berry, who had heard that a Habitat project was getting started in Nashville, attended his first meeting.

Bill had recently moved to the city from New York, and it just happens that he had been vitally involved there in renovating Habitat's six-story tenement on East Sixth Street. That evening, Nashville Habitat found their building committee chairman.

In the spring of 1983 in Burlington, Vermont, a talented young couple made a startling decision. Sally and Carty (short for Cartwright) Hall, both graduates of the University of Ohio at Athens, resolved to quit their jobs and step out in faith, volunteering a year of service with Habitat for Humanity. Carty, whose degree was in economics, enjoyed being a carpenter; Sally, an elementary school librarian, would take whatever work she could find to support them both.

The Halls asked Americus for a Habitat location somewhere in the eastern United States, since both their families were living in Ohio. But nothing seemed to work out. Each time they thought arrangements had been made with a project, for some reason the plans fell through.

Finally Ted Swisher put Sally and Carty in touch with a brand new and struggling Habitat group in Salem County, New Jersey. By this time the Halls had given notice at their jobs and their apartment both, and there was no choice about leaving! Locating Salem County on a road map, the Halls packed all their worldly goods in a U-Haul truck, and Carty started off. Sally followed in her ancient Volkswagen Bug, along with their two dogs and two cats.

It was October of 1983 when the Halls moved out in faith, knowing next to nothing about their destination. The Lord moved with them.

When Sally and Carty arrived in Salem County, one family had a welcoming meal waiting. Another offered the third floor of their farmhouse indefinitely, or until an affordable apartment could be found. A pastor and his wife made their garage available to store the Halls' belongings. A member of his congregation temporarily adopted the two cats, who didn't fit well into the augmented collection of dogs around the farmhouse. And Sally, who didn't really expect to find a job in her field at a time of year when teaching staffs were usually complete, was offered a position as an elementary school librarian *within three days.*

(Her interview for this job left her shaking her head. The superintendent of schools in the small district of Pennsville, New Jersey, turned out to be a longtime friend of Sally's former superintendent of schools in Burlington, Vermont. After one quick phone call between these two administrators, Sally knew she was hired.)

One afternoon a few weeks later, after Carty had put in a day's work on Salem County's first Habitat house, he stopped at the local Historical Society. His father had suggested, in a letter from Ohio, that Carty might unearth some interesting information in Salem.

Sure enough. Carty learned that an ancestor of his named William Hall, a carpenter by trade, had landed in Salem County from England some *306 years earlier,* in 1677. Carty discovered that in 1820, his great- great- great-grandfather, Edward Hall, another builder, had moved to Cincinnati (where Carty's family still lived). And he learned that a tiny cluster of houses known as Halltown still existed in Salem County just a few farms away from where he was staying.

When they first left Vermont, Sally and Carty Hall thought they were venturing into completely strange territory. They had never even heard of Salem County before they looked it up in the road atlas. But they moved out in faith, and followed the Lord's leading. And He led Carty right back to his roots.

Shortly after the Halls completed their year of volunteer service, their family's needs occasioned a move to Ohio. This time they packed up their two dogs and two cats and—yet another blessing from the Lord—their infant son.

The Halls also took along a great store of love. The Habitat folks in Salem County will always be grateful for this particular one of God's Incidents.

Finding your roots through Habitat has happened more than once, I've learned. In October 1985, when we held our fall board meeting in New York City, the culmination of our gathering was a huge march. Five hundred strong, carrying Habitat balloons and project banners from around the world, we walked on a glorious, crisp afternoon from St. James Cathedral in Brooklyn, where our meetings had been held, four miles across the Brooklyn Bridge to the six-story building renovated by Habitat on the Lower East Side. This first Habitat effort in the city was dedicated in a rousing, unforgettable service. Everyone present—local volunteers, Habitat supporters from all over, new homesteaders, famous folks like Jimmy and Rosalynn Carter and Andrew Young, along with unknown bystanders who were simply curious—went away with a realization that something exciting was happening on that street. The love and hard work of God's people had resulted in what one reporter called a "born-again slum."

Geoff and Dolores Van Loucks flew back to California that night, their euphoria still with them. Geoff, a member of our board of directors, and Dolores, who chaired the Habitat advisors, were both longtime super-supporters of the ministry.

A few days later Dolores visited Geoff's mother, Lenn Bragg, in a convalescent home, where she was recovering from a serious illness. Intensely interested in Habitat, Lenn asked all about the get-together in New York City. When Dolores described the big parade, her mother-in-law inquired where exactly the project was located.

"On East Sixth Street, near Avenue C," was the reply.

Lenn stared for a long moment. "That's where I was born!"

Geoff's grandparents had been immigrants from Scotland, and in 1911 Lenn was the first member of her family to be born in America. Seventy-four years later, her son and his wife had unknowingly returned to the site to celebrate the beginning of a new life for yet another generation of Americans. This stunning realization was one the Van Loucks family will not soon forget.

Habitat for Humanity became a reality in Americus in 1976. Our first headquarters building, which also served as my law office so that I could earn a living for my family, was an old house which we purchased for four thousand dollars. The Lord's hand was unquestionably in that acquisition, and the whole story is told in *Love in the Mortar Joints.*

As time passed and Habitat kept growing, we began to purchase other old dwellings in the neighborhood. Some were renovated for office space or volunteer housing; some could be repaired for sale to low-income families; others simply had to be razed for firewood, providing vacant land for new Habitat houses.

At one point we had an interest in acquiring three shacks which were near the Habitat office. We discovered that the owner was active in one of the large churches in Americus. So I got in touch with him to see if he would sell the shacks to us.

Within a few days he came to my office. Yes, he said, he was interested in selling those houses. I asked him the price. He quoted a figure that was, in my opinion, just about twice what the shacks were worth. I told him I thought the price was much too high, so he suggested that he owned other houses around town which might interest us. We got in his car and drove all over Americus, looking at probably twenty-five more shacks that he owned. Everytime we stopped at another dilapidated house, I would ask him how much he wanted, and he always quoted a price that was out of sight. We were not able to trade on anything.

A year went by. Then one day I received a telephone call. It was the owner of the shacks.

"Are you still interested in buying the three houses a block west of your office?"

"Certainly. But your price is just too high for us."

"What if I cut my price in half?"

"If you do that, I think we can make a deal. That's just about what the houses are worth. Why don't you stop by here at the office?"

Within a few minutes, the man appeared at my door. There was a smile on his face, and I knew there had to be a story behind his change of heart. I asked him about it.

"Well," he grinned a little sheepishly, "I have a married daughter who lives in Pennsylvania, and not very long ago I went up there to visit her. On Sunday I attended her church. The whole service was about Habitat for Humanity! They showed a slide presentation, and I began to realize that maybe I've been part of the problem. So I'm offering the three houses at half of my asking price."

At that point we shook hands. Habitat bought the shacks, and they have gradually been demolished and replaced by Habitat houses. The Lord moved in Pennsylvania, so that His children could move to decent homes in Georgia.

In April 1984 John and Ann Franken of Mulkiteo, Washington, went to Port Moresby, Papua New Guinea, to launch a new Habitat project. John had recently retired after thirty years as an executive behind a desk; furthermore, he had never particularly cared for working with his hands. But he and Ann were both convinced that the Lord had called them to this job. A few months after their arrival, John wrote a letter home about his experiences.

Where do you begin when you are supposed to start a new project? Since I plainly didn't know, I had to lean on the Lord more and more. There were days that I was certain I did not know enough to make the project come about, let alone make it a success! And in the process the Lord got me where He wanted me: not trusting in myself, or in the knowledge He had let me acquire, but in Him alone. Not a theoretical trust, but one where I had to go to Him every day with my practical problems.

In the very beginning we had to get to know our way around, finding out where to buy groceries and other necessities. We studied language every day. Then I began my research. I looked at what the government had done in housing. I tried to find out exactly who could not get a commercial bank loan. I wanted to know what the poor want in housing and what they can afford. I found material suppliers; I called on business executives to interest them in giving discounts on materials to build houses for the poor. I talked to the Labor Department to find out wage laws, and to the Building Department to learn about building codes and permit requirements.

One day I bought some drafting equipment and began drawing the first floor plan. Although I had done a fair amount of drafting in my life, I had never been involved in drawing structural details for a house. Once again I learned to lean heavily on the Lord. On the third try I finally came up with a house plan priced within the realm of possibility.

I took the drawings to the Building Engineer for a building permit. Explaining that I am not a builder or a draftsman of houses, I asked him to look over the drawings and red-line changes he wanted me to make. When I returned he informed me that the drawings had been approved exactly as submitted!

Initially I hired just two unskilled men, since at the first stage we were only making bricks from local soil mixed with cement. When we came to pouring the footing, we still had only unskilled labor. I had helped pour some concrete during orientation in Americus, so we managed. But when we had to lay bricks for the foundation wall, I did not have a bricklayer. Yes, I had laid some bricks during orientation, but there were always others around who really knew what they were doing. Without a bricklayer, the morning came that I had to do something. Out of the inner turmoil I felt, the Lord assured me that He wanted me to do it, and that He would bless the labors of my hands. So I started teaching the two hired men how to lay brick—a true case of the blind leading the blind! The foundation went up without any major trouble, and lo and behold, the finished work was level. When we started the walls, the Lord finally sent a bricklayer.

And so the house went up and was dedicated. It is truly a sermon in brick and mortar. It's a sermon testifying to God's love for poor people who need decent housing so desperately, but also testifying to His love for me. Often I have told the fellows in Pidgin, "Mi no masta; mi wokboi bilong Jisas Krais tasol." (I am not the boss; I am only a workman for Jesus Christ.)

The front cover of our dedication program proudly proclaimed: TO GOD BE THE GLORY. Even Ann does not fully realize how little I had to do with this first finished house. I have simply followed orders.

All my life I had told everybody that I was born with two left hands. Well, I believe that the Lord just chuckled at my attitude and said, "John, I did not create you with two left hands. I'll show you." And He did.

Habitat projects are always seeking funds—and always finding their needs supplied in unexpected ways. In 1982 the new Habitat group in Amarillo, Texas, was looking for land on which to build, and they had established three essential criteria. The location where they would launch their project had to be (1) affordable, (2) in an area that could be racially integrated, and (3) close to schools and public transportation.

After a lengthy search, the committee learned of an open tract of thirty-five lots, each valued at fifteen hundred dollars, in an area surrounded by four distinct groups: Anglo, Black, Hispanic, and Laotian. The land spread out along a main bus line and right across the street from an elementary school. The Habitat folks debated and prayed about how to proceed. Finally they decided to make an offer of five thousand dollars for four of the lots.

A few days later the reply came. The owner lived in California, but he had grown up in Amarillo. He told the committee that he had attended seminary as a young man, but then decided to enter business instead of the ministry. His ventures had succeeded, and now he would like to share some of his good fortune. For the five thousand dollars offered by Amarillo Habitat, he would deed them *all thirty-five building lots!*

The excited committee promptly named their newly-acquired land "Habitat Hill," and began planning homes for God's people. Shortly thereafter the city of Amarillo donated its services to lay out streets and sewer and water lines, and by this time the Habitat folks knew for sure that funds for building would be supplied. They were. Solid new homes are steadily going up in Amarillo, and Habitat Hill has become an ever-enlarging witness to the blessings of God.

Not every Habitat effort, of course, starts with a dollar, although many do.

In New Jersey, a gift of ten thousand dollars launched the Gloucester County project in 1986. These funds were raised a few dimes and quarters at a time, through sales of used clothing by women of the Pitman Baptist Church. They called their thrift shop, appropriately enough, *The Fig Leaf!*

My favorite story about a Habitat project with remarkable financial beginnings came from our affiliate in Tallahassee, Florida. Their president, Emory Hingst, pastor of St. Stephen's Lutheran Church there, related an unusual series of events.

Nineteen eighty-three was the year for First Presbyterian Church, Tallahassee, to celebrate its 150th anniversary. The congregation voted to undertake much-needed renovations to the worship area, built in 1838. However, there was a strong concern that building only for themselves would not be loving their neighbors. So the congregation decided that their capital campaign would include a request for contributions 25 percent above the total cost of renovation, with the additional funds to be used for service to the Tallahassee community. Since the original renovation estimate was $325,000, a large fund would become available to sponsor a community project. After careful consideration, the congregation decided to give this money to a local Habitat project—when one materialized. Other congregations were invited into the development of such a group. By the time Tallahassee Habitat for Humanity became a reality, their start-up fund from First Presbyterian Church came to more than $90,000!

After seven months of calling itself an organization and four months of being chartered by the State of Florida, Tallahassee Habitat decided it was ready to start building, with the promise of the money from First Presbyterian Church. However, we wanted to be good stewards and not spend money on land if we didn't have to. A friend of Habitat, Michele Archangeli, who leads Tallahassee Foundation (an organization to repair houses), introduced us to the City of Tallahassee's Department of Community Improvement.

Michele knew that this department was beginning a similar project, but would charge 4 percent interest. They had purchased three lots and had moved three condemned houses to them. We soon offered to make six living units on that site, through renovation and new construction. The city liked the idea, and we got the land for our first six housing units—for one dollar! We were ready to begin.

In order to put more money directly into building materials, I consulted a tax attorney friend of Habitat about obtaining a state tax exemption for our purchases. Since we live in the state capital, he gave me the name of a person who works for the state in such matters. He was friendly and helpful, but he didn't know whether we would qualify, and he said the paperwork would take at least three months. Ron Shaeffer, our diligent treasurer, thought it would be worth a try. He quickly filled out the forms and decided to walk them through, if he could, rather than send them in the mail.

On the way to the state office building, Ron forgot the name of the person and the particular office in which he was to start the process. Looking over the lengthy building directory in the lobby, he saw the name of a Habitat friend, Bebe Blount. Although her office was in a separate department of state government, he decided to see if he could use the telephone in her office, and to ask if she knew where he was supposed to go and whom he was to see. Bebe knew the head of the department; she walked Ron over to meet him; he said he thought he could help. In about twenty minutes, Ron walked out of the building with the exemption in his hand.

Ron called me immediately. He is usually fairly rational about spiritual matters—as I am—but that morning had him excited. Something different was happening.

Something different, indeed. When you move on faith, you'd better be ready to run to keep up with the Lord's leading. And along the way you'll discover that God's Incidents are not incidental at all.

14

Thank You, Jesus!

There is one exciting, unforgettable experience which comes to every Habitat project around the world. It happens each time another family moves into their new home. Probably I have been privileged to share in more of these memorable occasions than anyone else. I know that each one leaves me on a "Habitat high," and I return to my work with new energy and a stronger determination to conquer this problem of poverty housing.

It is difficult to convey in words the emotional impact experienced by a poor family when they have finally acquired a decent home. They have reached their impossible dream. But perhaps you can catch some of that excitement through their own words.

In July 1981 Cindy and Aaron Middlebrooks and their three children moved into the first Habitat house in Kansas City, Missouri.

I was looking everywhere for a house, because in our apartment all of the children had to sleep in one bedroom. I wanted a house for our family! My mother told me, "God has got something better for you." She said that to me after we failed to get a house we wanted to buy which was near our apartment. I couldn't see much hope. I kept praying, though.

One day I noticed the Habitat sign at Twenty-ninth and Paseo. I called the number. The lady on the phone said there was a long waiting list, but that she would send us an application form. I thought to myself, "There's no way we can get a house, because we don't make much money. We can't save enough to buy a house." I was getting ready to get depressed. But then I started looking up. We got the application, filled it out and sent it back. It was three months before we heard anything. Then one morning I got a call. I could have painted this city red, green, blue and yellow! I was so excited I couldn't stand it. They called me and said everything looks good, but they wanted to come over and talk to us. I ran and told all my friends. I called my mother. I called my friends at work. Everybody encouraged us. "You're gonna get it. You're gonna get it!" they said.

When they came over to our house that night, my husband was late. It seemed like everything was going wrong. At the end of the meeting, though, Rev. McGee said, "Pick out the house plans you want."

I asked Cindy how she felt when they finally moved in.

I was eight months pregnant. I was tired. That night it was unbelievable. I wanted to cry. Now we had something that was ours. It was beautiful. Windows open. No curtains up yet. Sheets were on the windows, but it was ours. I can't even express it. I'll never forget it. It was just like when I had my first baby. It's a feeling you can't express, but you never forget it. Oh boy! God sent us this house.

I love the Christian fellowship in Habitat for Humanity. I like the way the Habitat concept is helping people. That is God's plan for us. When Christ came, he didn't just come and do nothing. He helped everybody he came in contact with. We should do the same.

Five years after the Middlebrooks acquired their home, it was still a joy to them, and a witness to visitors who passed the gleaming, neatly landscaped dwelling on a busy boulevard in Kansas City. Aaron and Cindy are faithful Habitat volunteers who are helpful to newer homeowners. The Middlebrooks have caught the vision.

In the spring of 1984 we dedicated a new home in Americus for Diane Ellis. Diane and her family had moved out of an unpainted, uninsulated shack which Diane said was so cold in the wintertime they had to go outside to get warm. There was a single spigot near the back door for water.

As Habitat people and Diane's friends and neighbors crowded into her yard for the dedication service, she stepped to the microphone.

"I suppose all of you want to know how I feel about this new house," she said quietly. "Well, I'll tell you."

Suddenly Diane took a step backwards and began to jump up and down. "Yippee!" she yelled. "Yippee! Yippee!" Her arms were flailing wildly and she continued to yell. "Yippee! Yippee!" Finally she stopped. Everyone was laughing.

After a brief pause, she started jumping up and down once more, shouting even louder. "Yippee! Yippee! Yippee!" She stopped. Everyone laughed again, but more softly this time. And then she started jumping and yelling again. "Yippee! Yippee! Yippee!"

When Diane stopped jumping the third time, she was exhausted. Everyone in the yard was beginning to cry, and some minutes passed before we could resume the dedication. It was a powerful and magic experience.

Families have such strong feelings about their new houses not only because of the overcrowded or sub-standard situations they are leaving. They are also touched by the love and concern they experience from the Habitat people. In September 1984, when Charlotte, North Carolina, Habitat was dedicating two newly completed houses, a local television reporter asked one of the new homeowners, "What is your feeling about acquiring this new house in such an unusual fashion?"

She thought hard for a few moments. Then she replied, "The most wonderful part of it all was the realization that there were people who cared enough to make it possible."

Lonnie and Thelma Slaven have lived in Scott County, Tennessee, all their lives, except for a short time some years back when they moved to Dalton, Georgia, to look for work in the carpet mills. But when they discovered that their rent was consistently higher than their total income, they gave up and returned home. When they learned about Habitat, the Slavens lived in a 12-by-12-foot log house on a remote dirt road. Steep mountains surrounded their starkly beautiful hollow. Thelma cared for her six children, ages one to thirteen, without plumbing; a long extension cord entered the window from a neighbor's house, supplying power for a single light bulb and an old refrigerator. Uneven gaps between the logs were stuffed with old clothes and cardboard. If you left all the doors and windows open in your home in the middle of winter, you still would have a hard time imagining what the Slavens' cabin was like when the temperature reached -30F in January of 1985. Even with all the children in one bed, the littlest one, who always kicked the blankets off, nearly froze.

Lonnie Slaven was working from 3:30 P.M. to midnight in a nearby canvas factory. He earned $125 a week, with no insurance or fringe benefits. But he was thankful to have a job at all.

The family received a foodstamp allotment of $371 a month, which bought only the basics—beans, potatoes, flour, and meal. Every once in a while Thelma bought soda or candy for the children. But not often.

On November 2, 1985, Appalachia Habitat for Humanity gathered to dedicate the Slavens' new home. The four-bedroom, tightly insulated frame dwelling, built by volunteers and work groups from half a dozen states, covered 820 square feet. In order to make the house affordable there was no plumbing, but there was a kitchen sink and counters, and a room which had been designated to be a bathroom. Someday. Meanwhile the Slavens, after a down payment of $250, will make mortgage payments of $25 a month for eighteen years.

"At long last," said Thelma, "the children have a warm place to sleep. This house heats with a candle, it seems. And rain doesn't leak in anymore at night. We're so pleased to have a *house!*"

At the dedication service for every new Habitat house around the world, the homeowner is given a Bible, and everyone present shares in praising the Lord. The thanksgiving is scarcely a one-day phenomenon, however. I often remember a comment from Mrs. Savannah Simmons, who moved into the first Habitat house in Memphis, Tennessee.

"I'm so grateful to God for this house," she said, "every single morning I start praying in the front bedroom. Then I keep going right on through each room, thanking God for my house!"

Sometimes people are so full of emotion at the house dedication service that they simply cannot say anything. On the day before Easter in 1983 we gathered at Julia Battle's new house in Americus. Julia, a widow, had lived with two children and a ninety-six-year-old grandmother in an atrocious hovel; right in front of it, we built her new home. A few days after the dedication, the old shack was demolished, and Julia planted a garden in its place.

During the dedication service, Julia stepped to the microphone to speak. She dissolved in tears. For some minutes she tried unsuccessfully to compose herself. Finally she sat down. Throughout the rest of the service she never said a word, but she had already powerfully communicated her feelings to all of us who were privileged to be there.

When volunteers at the Pensacola, Florida, Habitat project had completed renovations on a house for Penny Hyde and her family, she poured out her appreciation in a moving letter:

Dear Habitat:

I'm not very good at preparing speeches or writing letters, so I can only speak from my heart.

Like so many in our world, I am a single parent with two small children—and not many support systems. For the past two years my life has suffered spiritual malnutrition. A feeling of 'death' was in my life—we survived the best way we could. Our home was a reflection of this same death. Either lack of necessary skills or money put a hold on making our home a healthy and happy place to be.

One day my mother handed me a brochure in which I came to know of Habitat for Humanity. From that day on, our lives were changed.

After being interviewed and accepted, the changes began. We now had a front door which we could actually lock; panes in broken windows to keep out the cold; a repaired roof; doors inside our house; paint donated for soot-ridden walls; a beautiful donated rug; and best of all, we could actually turn on faucets to have a decent bath, and broken pipes from the winter were repaired. Handmade cabinets were built to improve our kitchen. These are just a few things which you have done for us.

Beyond your loving services of time and caring in helping us reunite our home and family, Habitat for Humanity has also inspired again within my heart the purpose of our existence—to serve and love others.

Thanks again, Habitat, again and again. I would also like to give my "service of love" along with you, to help others the way you have given my family hope and love.

With much appreciation,
gratitude and love,

Penny, Aaron, and Nathan Hyde

On a snowy day in January of 1985 I rejoiced with the Box Elder Habitat folks at the dedication of their first house in Brigham City, Utah. Ray and Jan Meade and their three children had moved in a few weeks earlier, after waiting patiently for almost three years.

Ray had severe degenerative crippling arthritis, and most of his stomach had been surgically removed. He was always cold—he usually wore several shirts with a vest over them. He seemed to grow thinner and more hunched over every day. But from the day he found an advertisement in the newspaper for a lot which Habitat was able to purchase for a good price, Ray began to perk right up. He got so busy he seldom needed the vest any more. He never missed a day on the project site. He served coffee and homemade banana bread to the workers. He drove his pickup truck to haul supplies. He and Jan and the children helped every step of the way, from clearing the site of rocks in the beginning stages to painting and laying carpet as the house was completed.

By the time Ray's house was dedicated he had started gaining weight, and he stood straight and tall. The priest of the Meades' parish, Father Dan Charlton, gave the official message, and Ray responded briefly. He spoke softly, but his face glowed.

When the service was over, refreshments were offered. People were shoulder to shoulder in the small house. After a few moments, I saw an elderly man working his way through the crowd toward me. When he finally stood before me, he took my hand and squeezed it tightly. He said, "I'm Jan's father." He wanted to go on, but he broke down and began to cry. He continued to hold on to my hand for a long moment. I could see that he very much wanted to say more, but he couldn't compose himself. Finally he simply dropped my hand and walked away. "I'm Jan's father," is all he ever said, but it was enough.

The Meade family's monthly mortgage payment was well below their former rent for inadequate housing. Ray said making house payments was a real joy. He and Jan served on Box Elder Habitat's Family Selection and Support Committee, sharing their experience and concern with the next four families who had been chosen. The Meades never failed to contribute breads and handwork to Habitat bazaars and bake sales, and whenever they could, they brought an extra tithe of their house payment as a thank you to the Lord. The Meades had caught the vision, also.

As they suddenly find encouragement and hope, it is not unusual to discover that the health of new homeowners has improved dramatically. In 1985 I got a letter from Habitat partner Frank Basler of Tryon, North Carolina, describing a visit to the first homeowner in their Thermal Belt Habitat project.

Just to see Gwendolyn Miller in her new Habitat house is evidence of the power of God's love in action. She looks many years younger, and she is a picture of health. I recall the days sixteen months ago when she spent all day in bed and was convinced she would never live to see her house finished. When I asked her how she felt about her Habitat house, she responded in rapid bursts: "I love Habitat! I'm blessed! Thank the Lord! It no longer rains inside! Habitat should have been here long years ago!"

Not long after I heard from Frank Basler, another letter came from Bob Whitford, the dynamic professor at Purdue University who helped organize the Habitat project in Lafayette, Indiana. He was excited about a lot of "God's incidents" which kept happening to move their efforts ahead. But most thrilling of all, he said, was the partnership aspect of Habitat.

In a sense, redemption is occurring in front of our very eyes. The change in our first family (a single parent family with three teenage boys) is astonishing. Janie, the mother, is like a new person—brighter, cheerier, dressing and carrying herself more confidently. She no longer has to carry water four miles because the pipes are frozen, or live huddled up in two rooms of a dilapidated ten-room farmhouse. She seems to have renewed faith. Her three teenage sons are also behaving very differently. Tommy, the eldest, took on the drafting of the house plans by working after school with his drafting instructor. This from a boy whose interest in school had always been minimal. The whole family has been on the site working, and their attitude has been extremely infectious for the volunteers.

In early 1984 Pedro Castro Lopez, director of the Guatemala project, sent a report to the Americus office. After telling us that the first eighty-three houses in Phases I and II were completed, Pedro listed the families who had been chosen to receive the next seven houses:

1) Juan Vicente Mejia. Evangelical. He only has 2/9 of an acre.

2) Oscar Guillermo Velasquez Simon. Catholic. He does not have a house.

3) Antonio Ortiz Raymundo. Evangelical, attending Prince of Peace Church. They have ten people in their family and they live in a one room adobe house.

4) Jose Mendoza Raymundo. Evangelical, attending Central American Church. There are seven members of their family living on 5/9 of an acre. He earns $2 a day.

5) Pedro Lopez Castro. Evangelical, attending Central American Church. They live in a bamboo and straw house on their little farm of 4/9 acre. They raise garlic and make $700 a year.

6) Victorino Lopez Lopez. Traditional religion. He is a mason and makes $3.50 a day. He has 1/9 acre of land.

7) Gaspar Simon Marquin. Evangelical, attending Central American Church. Seven people are in the family. Income is $2 day. He has a tiny house of straw. The family has 8/9 acre of land.

When families like these have an opportunity to live in a permanent, solid home, which they will help to construct, their enthusiasm is boundless. During the most unsettled periods in recent years, when Habitat volunteers had to be temporarily evacuated, the Guatemalan families were making their own blocks, and despite ever-present danger and tragedy, the home building never stopped. During one of these times in 1982, we were not able to share in the dedication of the new house of Jose Mendoza Ailon. But when he and his family left once and for all their pitiful shack in Aguacatan, we learned of Jose's feelings in a memorable letter to our Overseas Projects Director Bob Stevens, who had founded the Guatemala project.

I write you greeting you in the name of our great God, hoping that God showers blessings on you and your family. We here, thanks to God, find ourselves quite well at this time. We are in good health, waiting to see how the situation goes, which appears to be improving considerably. After this greeting, I go on to say, God will pay you and the other brothers of Habitat, for helping us. We are now in our new house. We are very content. It is finished, and today I send you, brother in Christ, our thank you. Continuing to help others, we here will follow the Lord to the end. We are praying for you; we beg you to pray for us also. Until we see each other, my greetings to you all again. I close not saying goodbye, but until shortly.

Half a world away, Citoyen Kisidika in Kinshasa, Zaire, expressed his gratitude to the Almighty for his home, "We moved from a two-room hovel in the slums to a new Habitat house. Today my family is happy and healthy, and we can face life with dignity. We praise God for His great love. Thank you, Habitat friends, for giving life to my family."

I would be less than honest if I conveyed the impression that, after struggling with shortages of funds and volunteers, and oversupplies of red tape and roadblocks, when a Habitat family finally moves in, everyone invariably lives happily ever after. Actually, when a project completes a home, the work is nowhere near finished.

The most important follow-up job any Habitat group has to do, of course, is to make sure house payments keep coming in. Without them, the whole system breaks down. Ingenious measures have been employed at several locations, to encourage homeowners to be faithful with their mortgage payments.

In Kenya, a large sign was placed in front of the twenty-first house:

THIS HOME IS BEING BUILT
WITH HOUSE PAYMENTS ONLY

It soon became clear to the whole area that if mortgage income to the project slowed down, so did work on this home.

In Haiti, when payments from a number of families failed to appear, volunteer Art Russell convened a meeting to announce that the project would close for lack of funds. Within a couple of months, pressure from the families still waiting for their homes to be built had convinced the others to get back on schedule, and construction resumed.

In Mbandaka, Zaire, the Habitat committee found yet another effective collection method: The names of homeowners whose payments were in arrears were read over a local radio station!

Certainly, the best way to insure the receipt of regular house payments is through an educational process which communicates the whole Habitat philosophy. Habitat families have never before experienced the complicated demands which accompany the responsibility of home ownership. To ease this transition—and to avoid the foreclosures which are often part of government housing programs—every Habitat project has a committee to work with the new homeowners on a continuing basis. This group, which includes representatives from all segments of the local effort, makes a strong personal commitment to each family over as many years as may be necessary.

In Chicago, the Habitat committee, through meetings, home visits, workshops, and a great deal of prayer, managed to solve some serious difficulties in their own situation, and at the same time to evolve an effective program for helping families become successful homeowners. Chicago Habitat emphasizes three areas, all of which are crucial in any project.

1. *Financial management.* Habitat cannot take over a family's finances, but general principles of budgeting can be offered. New homeowners need assistance as they encounter a maze of paperwork and bills, and the unexpected requirements of insurance and property taxes.

2. *Interpersonal skills.* Habitat can help families learn to live side by side, to resolve conflict, and often to be joint owners of a building.

3. *Home ownership skills.* Many people who have never owned a home have also never planted a tree or a garden, fixed a leaky pipe, or caulked a window. Home maintenance can be learned. And the Habitat homeowner, gradually needing to call for help and advice less often, is also acquiring the exhilarating feeling of pride that comes from personal competence and independence.

It may take years of effort on both sides before the partnership can be judged to have succeeded. But when it does, the homeowning family, through their house payments and their contributions of time and skills and money, will in turn be playing a significant role in providing still more families in need with that exciting commodity—a new home.

A new home. For many of us in Western countries that simply means moving from one solid middle-class structure to another, probably a fancier one in a different location. To a Habitat family anywhere, a new home means much more.

It means being able to come in out of the cold and the rain and the bugs. It means not having to move suddenly because the rent has been raised, and it means knowing that the children can go to the same school next year that they attended this year. As one homeowner told me feelingly, it means that "The kids aren't ashamed now to have their friends find out where they live." Most of all, it means hope.

The first house that Koinonia Partners ever built, back in 1969, was for Bo and Emma Johnson. Their family lived across the road from Koinonia in a shack that had no plumbing or insulation. A few light bulbs hung from exposed wires. Bo, a tenant farmer, had never been able to go to school; Emma had finished tenth grade.

A solid concrete block house was built for their family at a cost of six thousand dollars. A very simple home, it was nevertheless a palace compared to their old shack. It included a modern kitchen, a good heating system, and an indoor bathroom. The Johnsons' monthly payment was set at twenty-five dollars.

When Bo and Emma moved in on their son Junior's birthday, November 11, 1969, one of their daughters, Mattie Pearl, was ten. Everyone called her "Cookie." She was bright and ambitious, and determined she would finish high school. When she did, I helped her get a partial scholarship to Tougaloo College in Mississippi.

Exactly fifteen years after her family moved into their new home, Cookie entered my office in Americus. She was beaming.

"Guess what, Millard?"

"What, Cookie?"

"I've just graduated from law school!"

Cookie is now a member of the Bar in Washington, D.C. She also has served on the board of directors of Koinonia Partners. Her younger sister, Sally, graduated from Mercer University in Macon, Georgia, and is working as a psychologist in Washington, D.C. Another sister is an LPN. Bo and Emma, who have faithfully made their payments to the Fund for Humanity all these years, are justly proud of their family. And their house is also bright and attractive!

Back in 1982, when Linda and I made a return visit to Ntondo, Zaire, we were treated to a tumultuous welcome. The Habitat project there was well along toward the goal of three hundred houses—one for every family in the village. The celebration, featuring drum-beating, singing, dancing, and lots of flowers as well as flowery speeches, included a brief welcome by a student who had been specially chosen for the occasion. I particularly remember a few sentences, because in not very many words, Mong'elo Komba-Ilongo managed to say a great deal. Smiling, he addressed the crowd.

> We have much happiness in our hearts today. And this happiness of ours will have no end, on top of the love God has given us. Before you came, we never thought that we would have a helper filled with the love of God. But today we sleep and eat and live in decent houses we never dreamed of before. All of this only because of God's love!

Mong'elo had caught the vision. All of these houses happen only because of God's love.

In all my years with Habitat, I'm sure that there is no one whose reaction to their new home touched me any more deeply than did Annie Wofford's.

In March of 1980 I took Mary Lou Brown, who was then a newspaper editor in Plains, Georgia, to visit Annie in her shack in Americus at 1105 Quincy Alley. Annie's husband had walked out years before. The house, displaying gaping holes in the ceilings and floors, had no water, no bathroom—not even an outside privy. One fireplace was the only source of heat.

"When it rains, we can't find anywhere to stay," Annie told us matter-of-factly. "When the wind blows outside, it blows clothes and things all over the house. We used to have two fireplaces, but one of the chimneys fell down. We just all bundle up under quilts in the cold spells."

Annie had recently learned that Habitat volunteers were going to build her a new home. It would be constructed on the same site, and the present shack would be dismantled and put to the one use it was really good for: firewood to heat the new house. "And we're going to have a bathroom and a kitchen—with water!" Annie kept repeating that she could hardly believe it.

As we left this pathetic dwelling, in which Annie struggled to maintain a home for her five boys, ages five to eleven, the newspaper editor was weeping.

A short time later, without saying a word to anyone, Annie wrote to the newspaper, and her letter was printed in the edition of April 4, 1980. I will never forget her message.

Dear Jesus,

I love you with all my heart. I thank you for saving my soul. You changed me from my wicked ways. I thank you for bringing me through my ups and downs.

Sometimes I couldn't sleep at night for worrying about where me and my children was going to get our next meal from. Thank you, Jesus, for making a way for us. My pastor told me to come to his home, but I knew he had his family to see after.

I thank you, Jesus, for being a father to my children, because their father don't care for them. He won't do nothing for them. But Jesus, you been there as a father and a mother, and I thank you for sending your people to me, who are blessing me and my children with a new house. I know it was you, Jesus, nobody but you. I thank Jesus for Habitat. . . .

Will you print this in your paper for me? I know some people are going to think I'm crazy, but I am crazy for Jesus, and I thank you, Jesus.

Annie Ruth Wofford
Americus, Georgia

We thank *you*, Annie.

15

A Conscience for the World

n January of 1985, I was in the middle of a jampacked speaking trip across California. I had already spoken in eight cities, and I was being driven between Stockton and Santa Rosa by Vern Robertson, a retired Presbyterian pastor. Vern had taken early retirement because of a health problem, but that had now improved considerably, and he was anxious to talk with me about the possibility of volunteer service with Habitat. As we drove north through spectacular countryside dotted with lush vineyards, Vern threw a series of questions at me in rapid succession.

Suddenly he asked one I hadn't heard before. "Millard, what is your vision of what Habitat will become in the years ahead?"

Four years earlier, I had been asked a similar significant question—interestingly enough, by another Californian. But that query concerned Habitat's *goal*. This was something different: what was Habitat *becoming?*

I thought about Vern's question for a minute. Then it just came to me.

"I envision Habitat for Humanity becoming *the conscience of the world concerning shelter.*"

I pondered my own response. I knew God had given it to me. Wow—this is the means by which our goal can be achieved!

Habitat, I realized, must put the idea of shelter for all of God's people into the mind and heart of every person in a way that will compel action. We must educate consciences. We must publicize the need, promote the goal, and provide the opportunity for change in so many ways that poor housing will become unacceptable, and good housing will become a matter of conscience.

That will be an enormous task. But we can do it.

I was raised in Alabama. My mother died when I was very young. My dad remarried, though, and we had a Christian home. We went to church all the time—Sunday morning, Sunday night, and on Wednesday night for prayer service. We were churchgoing folks! My daddy was a good man. We had a good family. But I never had my conscience educated about poverty.

During my growing-up years, the definition I learned of what really constituted a true believer in Jesus Christ went like this. At some point in your life a preacher stood up in the front of the church and said, "Accept Christ," and you decided to walk down the aisle and tell him you were sorry for your sins. After that, depending on whether you were a Methodist or a Baptist, you got a little water or a whole lot put on you, and then you could no longer fish on Sunday. If you were married, you couldn't run around openly with other women. You couldn't get drunk in public. You couldn't play ball or attend a ball game on Sunday. (Playing ball on Sunday was one of the worst sins.) And you couldn't have a whole lot of enjoyment riding around in a car on Sunday afternoon. That was close to being a sin. You had to go to church regularly—at least three services a week. There were some other things sort of thrown in there, but finally, to be a real *sanctified* Christian, you had to develop a ministerial tone to your voice. When that occurred, you were a true believer.

But being a Christian didn't have anything to do with the poor. Nothing. My conscience never got educated about the poor when I was growing up. And I have observed, as I have traveled around this country, that there are still an awful lot of people whose consciences have not been educated on this subject. If you read the Bible carefully, however, you will be forced to conclude that God has a special concern and a special love for the poor.

Can you say that you are a disciple of Jesus, living on one side of town in affluence, if there are people on the other side of town who do not have a decent place to live, or a good roof over their heads, or a solid floor under their feet, or insulation in their walls—and you are unwilling to go across town and do something about those conditions? *We need our consciences educated.* One of the most frequent comments we hear from people who go on Habitat for Humanity work camps is that when they return home they see things they never saw before!

Anyone can join our conscience-educating partnership. We offer petitions and bulletin inserts for the Day of Prayer and Action, bumper stickers, brochures, slide presentations—and of course we have lots more copies of *Bokotola, Love in the Mortar Joints,* and *No More Shacks!* We have organized fundraising and conscience-raising walks to Indianapolis in 1983, Kansas City in 1986, and Atlanta in 1988.[1] You can come along, or organize your own. Or, like many other Habitat folks, you might plan a bike ride, a concert, a marathon, a bowl-a-thon, a rock-a-thon, or some other thon![2]

Wherever you go, there are opportunities. I ride in dozens of airplanes every year. I never know who will be sitting beside me, but I do know this: by the time our wheels touch down at the next airport, my seatmate will have heard about Habitat for Humanity. At some point, our conversation will have centered on the worldwide need for housing. And it's just possible that this person will go home seeing things that were never noticed before.

A few years ago I was on a speaking trip in Tupelo, Mississippi, before a Habitat project had been formed there. On this occasion, I went at the invitation of Curtis Petrey, a United Methodist pastor who had a circuit of rural churches near Tupelo. There are some great little towns around Tupelo with names like Algoma, Pontotoc, and Palestine. I spoke in all these places on Saturday and Sunday. On Monday morning I was having breakfast with Curtis and his wife, Nancy, when the phone rang. Curtis answered it. After a brief conversation he returned and sat down, with a big smile on his face.

"Millard," he said, "you'll be interested to know what that call was about. A man who heard you in church yesterday called to say that when he walked out of his house this morning he saw that the house across the street was in pitiful condition. He said he had never noticed it before, and he was so upset he went to his next-door neighbor—who was also in church yesterday—and asked if he had noticed the condition of the house across the street. The neighbor looked over there and said that he really hadn't seen it, either. They both went right over. There's a widow living there on a very limited income; the house is leaking; the walls are falling in; the floor is collapsing. This man was calling to tell me they are both staying out of work today to get started on repairing her house!"

There are many ways to educate consciences. First and foremost, Habitat for Humanity is in the business of providing shelter. But because Habitat folks are always concerned about the whole person, a remarkable number of related ministries have developed. And each one offers important reminders of what we are about.

In Milledgeville, Georgia, Habitat for Handicapped Humanity was founded by Joe and Stephanie Thomas. This group seeks to provide funds and specific advice whenever affiliate projects are building homes for disabled persons.

In New York City, a casual comment by project director Rob DeRocker on a local radio show launched an all-out drive called Operation Sleeping Bag. Since then, hundreds of people who were homeless or living in unheated rooms, have obtained a warm sleeping bag from Habitat, "sold" to them in accordance with the economics of Jesus. Obviously, a sleeping bag is no substitute for a decent house; but it can make the difference between life and death—or frostbite—on a winter night. And as a result of this effort, some of the homeless have been motivated to work as volunteers in the New York project.

In Americus, boxes of used eyeglasses pour into our office every day. These are sorted, packaged, and shipped in fifty-five-gallon drums to Habitat locations in Africa, South America, and Papua

New Guinea where eyeglasses are not readily available. Sold at minimal cost, eyeglasses which would otherwise be discarded are recycled to fill a critical need. At the same time, when every pair in a drum has been sold, the proceeds will build another house!

There are many other organizations which are helping with conscience-raising on the issue of shelter. Beginning in 1987, the United Nations is sponsoring the observance of the International Year of Shelter for the Homeless. This emphasis will continue until the end of the century. Worldwide plans and programs have been in the works for a long time, in order to highlight—and attack—this problem on an international scale. As Christians, we need to be saying *"Right on!"* and supporting this effort, making more people aware, and motivating them to act.

The campaign to educate the consciences of the world demands an ever-enlarging partnership, and whenever Habitat for Humanity can join forces with other groups, we do so. World Vision has supplied Habitat with several portable sawmills, crucial equipment in projects overseas. In the United States, in addition to their partnership with us in the Mississippi delta, World Vision has helped to underwrite work groups of federal prisoners in Habitat projects all over the country, in cooperation with Prison Fellowship. Under the internationally known Prison Fellowship program, founded by Charles Colson, groups of Christian prisoners are furloughed to spend one or two weeks building on Habitat projects and living in local homes.[3] In 1985, we welcomed volunteers from the American Jewish Society for Service, who worked for seven weeks at the Amarillo, Texas, project. The West German Church Agency Vereinigte Evangelische Mission (United Evangelical Mission), headquartered in Wuppertal, has supported Zaire Habitat projects with funds and volunteers. And the search for other agencies who would like to work with us continues.

We are grateful for the ways the partnership is growing. Sometimes, in fact, it grows so rapidly that new supporters don't really know the whole story. On one occasion John and Harriet Bates, Habitat friends from Americus, returned after a vacation trip to Milwaukee with an experience they couldn't wait to tell us. One evening, they said, they were having dinner with their hosts in Wisconsin, when the subject of Habitat for Humanity came up.

Their friends, who had recently gotten involved with the new affiliate there in Milwaukee, were surprised. "You mean you have a Habitat in *Americus?*"

It doesn't really matter whether the Bates' friends had the whole story. What does matter is that their consciences had been touched, and that as a result they were doing something about poor housing.

That same something continues to happen all around the world. And every house we build, every crumbling dwelling we rehabilitate, every residence we repair is a sermon. It becomes a sign of God's love to all who live there, and to all who walk by. Each of these homes is like a conscience, reminding both builder and resident that substandard housing *can* be eliminated.

Habitat is exploding in so many directions, and in such exciting ways, that it's difficult, even in our international office in Americus, to keep track of all the developments. In 1980, when *Love in the Mortar Joints* was published, there were fewer projects in the entire United States (eleven) than there were five years later in a single state! By 1995 we expect to have Habitat projects in more than a thousand locations in this country, and others in at least fifty countries overseas.

In every location, whether in the United States or overseas, as new homeowners make house payments into the local "Fund for Humanity," the money is recycled and the effort expands. Each family is encouraged to help others, through accelerating their payments, if possible, and by donating their time and labor. Habitat's program is no "giveaway." We believe in the dignity of each person, and we always want to help in a way that is uplifting and strengthening, never in a way that is demeaning, or which fosters dependency.

Furthermore, the Habitat concept can succeed anywhere. There are just three essential criteria.

First, there must be a core group of dedicated Christian leaders at each project location, partners who will faithfully apply the economics of Jesus in dealing with His people in need. Second, the families who have been selected must be involved in the actual process of building their own house and the houses of others. Third, there must be love in the mortar joints—genuine Christian love manifested toward the families receiving the houses.

We already have much to celebrate. My heart is full of joy,

not only about the miracle of Habitat for Humanity, but also about the rewarding life Linda and I have together. Ever since our reconciliation in New York City many years ago, we have felt blessed and led by the Lord. And on an evening in New York in August 1985, at the close of our second work camp with President Carter, Linda and I experienced a profound benediction, and a clear sign from heaven that we must continue on the path God has shown us.

We had finished supper at the Metro church, and we decided to walk to Times Square to see a movie. *Back to the Future* was showing at a theater on Broadway. In this science fiction comedy, a teenager is suddenly thrust twenty years back in time, and he encounters his future parents in their high school. Both of us thoroughly enjoyed the film. The story was fun, but on another level it was, for us, highly symbolic. As we left the theater, we went "back to the future" ourselves, remembering a time in New York City twenty years before.

It was November, and cold, that night in 1965. Our personal future was very much in doubt. Linda had left me some weeks earlier. She was considering a divorce. While she was in New York, there had been a big blackout, which was as dark as our relationship at that moment. I eventually pursued her from our home in Montgomery, Alabama. One evening, Linda and I went to see another movie, *Never Too Late*. The title proved prophetic. A few hours later we were finally able to confess the many ways in which we had betrayed each other and God, and out of that confession came a flood of tears, and the beginning of reconciliation. It wasn't too late. That night we decided to leave our business, give our money away, and seek God's new direction for our lives.

Now, twenty years later, we had returned to the place which had so much significance for us. When the movie ended, we walked over to Fifth Avenue, and then to Saint Patrick's Cathedral. We had sat on the steps there on that cold night in 1965, and then made our life-changing decision. As we walked across Fifth Avenue at Fiftieth street, after a twenty-year interval, Linda suddenly exclaimed, "There's the moon!"

I looked up in awe. In a perfectly clear sky, a full moon was dead center over Fiftieth street. For a while we just stood on the corner and stared. At last we walked on slowly, to the steps of the cathedral. For fifteen minutes or so we sat there, reminiscing about the last time we had sat in that spot, and about all that had happened in the intervening years. As we left, we vowed that we would come back to those steps for another talk, after twenty more years.

It was slightly less than two decades ago that a few people at Koinonia Farm began talking about building a lot of houses for God's people in need. In 1968 our dream to eliminate poverty housing in Sumter County, Georgia, sounded awesome. Incredible.

As this book goes to press in 1986, the work crews from Habitat for Humanity and Koinonia Partners have completed more than two hundred new houses in Sumter County and repaired and renovated many others. Our dream no longer sounds impossible. And now we have set our sights much higher. We plan to eliminate poverty housing from the face of the earth.

It can happen. If people of goodwill everywhere will join us in this great task, it can happen. If each one of you whose conscience has been educated will in turn educate others, it can happen. Every person in the world can have at least a simple, decent house to live in. Help us make that happen.

Join with us, under the banner of Habitat for Humanity or under some other banner. In whatever way the Lord leads you, enable someone to escape from sleeping in a crumbling mud hut or a rotting city slum or a cardboard box, or perhaps only on the ground or a cement sidewalk. We are involved in a magnificent partnership, with each other and with God. We can succeed.

Sam Mompongo, the dynamic Habitat project director in Ntondo, Zaire, once made a statement to me which describes our current situation perfectly.

"The problem of housing in the world is not poor people," said Sam. "It is people poor in faith."

No more shacks! No poverty housing in the whole world! Ridiculous? Outrageous? Impossible?

Of course not. *With God, all things are possible.*

1   Janet Morton, a nursing instructor at Georgia Southwestern College, made the first pledge to our walk to Indianapolis to raise a hundred thousand dollars. Three years later when we were planning a longer walk to Kansas City to raise a million dollars, Janet eagerly offered again to make the first pledge—and then sent ten times the amount. Our walk to Atlanta will have a goal of ten million dollars. We'll be sure to contact Janet first!

2   In 1985 Habitat formed a development office to coordinate fundraising efforts in all areas, and Tom Ford, a Lutheran pastor from Fort Collins, Colorado, became our first director. If you come up with a fresh and effective fundraising idea which other Habitat supporters might use, we would appreciate your sending the details to: Director of Development, Habitat and Church Streets, Americus, Georgia 31709.

3   Habitat South Director Luther Millsaps has established a similar program in the Mississippi Delta, working with county and state prisoners. Each morning, prisoners are released to work on a Habitat house; in the evening, they return to their cells. As they learn new skills, these men are also exposed to Christian love. "Several of the prisoners," says Luther, "have professed Christ because of their experiences."

Left: Ten years later
. . . the first Habitat
house built in San
Antonio, Texas, in
1976.

Right: A new
Habitat house
goes up in
Charlotte,
North Caro-
lina.

THESE HOMES ARE BEING
BUILT BY IHH AND SOLD
ON A NON-PROFIT, NON-
INTEREST BASIS. NO TAX
MONEY IS BEING USED.
THIS WORK IS MADE
POSSIBLE BY THE ENERGIES
AND RESOURCES OF
CONCERNED CHRISTIANS.

IMMOKALEE
HABITAT FOR
HUMANITY, INC.

Project director
Jose Brueggen and
his wife, Charo, in
Immokalee, Florida
—site of one of Hab-
itat's first projects in
the United States.

Left: A Habitate president, Duane Yoder, helps Brenda and Beverly Yommer place a Bible in the cornerstone of their new house in Garret County, Maryland.

Proud homeowners Arthur and Bernice Whitaker *(left)* and their five foster children moved into the first Habitat house in Salem County, New Jersey. An ecstatic Diane Ellis *(right)* jumps for joy at the dedication of her new house.

Right: Venice and Michael Bates and three of their five children thank volunteers at their house dedication in Atlanta as Habitat board member Bonnie O'Neal looks on.

Habitat for Humanity volunteers turn a dilapidated old shack *(above)* into a solid, beautiful, pride-generating house in Waynesburg, Pennsylvania *(below)*.

Linda and Millard Fuller

"All of God's people should have at
least a simple, decent place to live."

Appendix A

Official Purposes of Habitat for Humanity, Inc.

The official purposes of Habitat for Humanity are to sponsor specific projects in habitat development globally, starting with the construction of modest but adequate housing, and to associate with other groups functioning with purposes consistent with those of Habitat, as stated in the Articles of Incorporation, namely:

1. To witness to the gospel of Jesus Christ throughout the world by working in cooperation with God's people in need to create a better habitat in which to live and work.
2. To work in cooperation with other agencies and groups which have a kindred purpose.
3. To witness to the gospel of Jesus Christ through loving acts and the spoken and written word.
4. To enable an expanding number of persons from all walks of life to participate in this ministry.

Guidelines for implementing the above purposes are as follows:

1. Believing that the work of Habitat for Humanity is inspired by the Holy Spirit, we understand the purposes express the hope that others may be grasped and led in yet unforeseen ministries by the Holy Spirit.
2. The term *in cooperation* used in Habitat's stated purposes should be defined in terms of *partnership*.
3. *Adequate housing* as used in the purposes means housing, but much more, including total environment; e.g., economic development, compassionate relationships, health, energy development, etc.
4. *Partnership* implies the right of all parties to engage in vigorous negotiation and the development of mutually agreed-upon goals and procedures. The negotiation in partnership should occur at each project and will include such items as defining what adequate housing means in that particular project, who are God's needy, and what local entity will control the project.

5. *Partnership* further implies that all project personnel—local people or expatriate volunteers—have a primary relationship to the local committee in regard to all matters relating to that particular project.
6. A primary concern in all matters is respect for persons, including their culture, visions, and dignity. Habitat's stance is one of responding to expressed needs of a people in a given area who are seeking a relationship of *partner* with Habitat for Humanity.
7. All Habitat projects must establish a Fund for Humanity, and financing of houses and other ventures must be on a noninterest basis. Each Fund for Humanity will be funded through voluntary gifts, both in cash and in kind, grants, interest-free loans, all from individuals, churches, other groups, and foundations. All repayments from houses or other Habitat-financed ventures will also be returned to the local Fund for Humanity. Finally, Habitat projects may operate enterprises which will generate funds for the local Fund for Humanity.

Appendix B

Maps of Habitat Projects

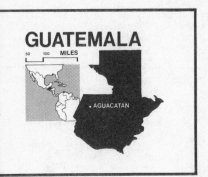

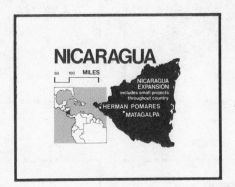

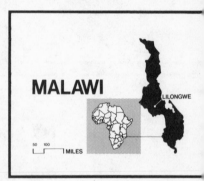

GEMENA
BASANKUSU
MBANDAKA
LAKE TUMBA EXPANSION
NTONDO
KINSHASA
KIKWIT

MILES
50 100

ZAIRE

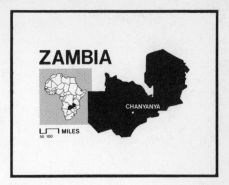

ZAMBIA

CHANYANYA

MILES
50 100

INDIA

50 100
MILES

KHAMMAM

BALINTOCATOC

PHILIPPINES

50 100
MILES

PAPUA NEW GUINEA

TUMUNG

PORT
MORESBY

50 100
MILES

TEMOTU PROVINCE

50 100
MILES

SOLOMON ISLANDS

● AFFILIATED PROJECTS

★ REGIONAL/NATIONAL CENTERS

1 Guatemala

2 Nicaragua

3 Haiti

4 Peru

5 Bolivia

6 Zaire

7 Uganda

8 Zambia

9 Kenya

10 India

11 Papua New Guinea

12 Burundi

13 Malawi

14 Tanzania

15 Philippines

16 Solomon Islands

Appendix C

Regional and National Centers

Regional Centers

Habitat Northeast

Connecticut	N. New Jersey
Maine	New York
Massachusetts	Rhode Island
New Hampshire	Vermont

Ron & Barbara Yates
P.O. Box 322
Acton, MA 01720
(617) 889–8604 (Work)
   264–0353 (Office)

Habitat Mid-Atlantic

Delaware	S. New Jersey
Maryland	N. Virginia
Pennsylvania	Washington, D.C.
	West Virginia

Woody & Penny Jenkins
80 Buckshire Drive
Holland, PA 18966
(215) 357–9220

Habitat South Atlantic

North Carolina	E. Tennessee
South Carolina	S. Virginia

Sandra Graham
P.O. Box 624
Easley, SC 29640
(803) 855–1102

Habitat Southeast

Florida	Georgia

Ted Swisher
Habitat & Church Streets
Americus, GA 31709
(912) 924–6935

Habitat South

Alabama	Mississippi
Louisiana	W. Tennessee

Luther Millsaps
P.O. Box 854
Tupelo, MI 38802
(601) 844–2397 (Office)
   844–2906 (Home)

Habitat Mideast

Ohio	Indiana
	Kentucky

Hubert & Fran Ping
Route 1, Box 86A
Thorntown, IN 46071
(317) 325–2516

Habitat Midwest

Illinois	Minnesota
Iowa	North Dakota
Michigan	South Dakota
	Wisconsin

Jim Carr
4 Indian Drive
Clarendon Hills, IL 60514
(312) 458–4100 (Office)
   325–1528 (Home)

Habitat of the Ozarks

Arkansas	Missouri
Kansas	Nebraska

Rae Johnson
3203 North National
Springfield, MO 65803
(417) 833–0103

Habitat Southwest

Texas   Oklahoma

Mary Brock
6740 Harvest Glen
Dallas, TX 75248
(214) 661–5709

Rocky Mountain Habitat

Colorado   New Mexico
Idaho   Utah
Montana   Wyoming

Mary Elizabeth Schumacher
750 Eleventh Street
Boulder, CO 80302
(303) 442–9077

Habitat West

Alaska   Hawaii
Arizona   Nevada
California   Oregon
                Washington

Gene Crumley
P.O. Box 901
Santa Cruz, CA 95061
(408) 426–2010 (Work)
      427–0965 (Home)

National Center

Habitat Canada

George Anderson
P.O. Box 135
Thornhill, Ontario L3T 3N1
    or
R.R. #3 Vivian Side Road
Newmarket, Ontario L3Y 4W1
(416) 889–0172 (Office)
      895–7785 (Home)

Appendix D

Habitat for Humanity Project Locations

Habitat for Humanity projects are either sponsored or affiliated. *Sponsored projects* receive both funds and personnel from Habitat International. *Affiliated projects* follow Habitat for Humanity guidelines, but the responsibility for generating funds and recruiting personnel rests with a local committee. *Regional* and *national centers* assist the affiliate projects within their geographical region and help promote the worldwide work of Habitat.

Sponsored Projects

Bolivia
Alto Beni
Burundi
Gitega
Guatemala
Aguacatan
Haiti
Dianeville
Dumay
Saint Marc (2 projects)
India
Khammam
Kenya
Nzoia Community
Malawi
Lilongwe
Nicaragua
Nicaragua Expansion
German Pomares
Matagalpa
Papua New Guinea
Port Moresby
Tumung

Peru
Juliaca
Manazo
Puno
Philippines
Balintocatoc
Solomon Islands
Temotu Province
Tanzania
Kasulu
Uganda
Gulu
Zaire
Basankusu
Gemena
Kikwit
Kinshasa
Lake Tumba Expansion
Mbandaka
Ntondo
Zambia
Chanyanya

Affiliated Projects

Alabama
Shoals Habitat for Humanity (Florence)
Arizona
Maricopa County Habitat for Humanity (El Mirage/Sun City)
Tucson Habitat for Humanity

California
Contra Costa County Habitat for Humanity (Pittsburg)
Habitat for Humanity Fresno
Habitat for Humanity of Sonoma County (Santa Rosa)
Habitat for Humanity of Ventura

Sacramento Habitat for Humanity
San Joaquin Habitat (Stockton)

Colorado
Denver Habitat for Humanity

Connecticut
Habitat for Humanity of Greater
Bridgeport

Florida
Habitat for Humanity of Greater Or-
lando Area
Habitat for Humanity Manasota
(Sarasota)
Habitat for Humanity of Broward
(Fort Lauderdale)
Immokalee Habitat for Humanity
Lee County Habitat for Humanity
(Fort Myers)
Pensacola Habitat for Humanity
Pinellas Habitat for Humanity (St.
Petersburg)
South Brevard Habitat for Human-
ity (Melbourne)
Tallahassee Habitat for Humanity

Georgia
Americus Habitat for Humanity
Atlanta Habitat for Humanity
Cartersville-Bartow County Habitat
for Humanity (Cartersville)
Coastal Empire Habitat for Human-
ity (Savannah)
Cobb County Habitat for Humanity
(Marietta)
Columbus Area Habitat for Human-
ity
Habitat for Humanity of Rome and
Floyd Counties (Rome)
Habitat for Humanity of Northeast
Georgia (Clarkesville)
Henry County Habitat for Humanity
(McDonough)
Macon Area Habitat for Humanity
Monroe County Habitat for Human-
ity (Forsyth)
North Central Georgia Habitat for
Humanity (Ellijay)
Peach Area Habitat for Humanity
(Fort Valley)

Thomasville-Thomas County Habitat (Thomasville)

Illinois
East St. Louis Habitat for Humanity
Habitat for Humanity of Danville
Habitat for Humanity of McLean
County (Bloomington)
Metro-Chicago Habitat for Human-
ity

Indiana
Habitat for Humanity of Boone
County (Lebanon)
Habitat for Humanity of Evansville
Habitat for Humanity of Lafayette

Iowa
Des Moines Habitat for Humanity:
S.H.E.L.T.E.R.

Kansas
Topeka Habitat for Humanity

Kentucky
Ashland-Ironton Area Habitat for
Humanity (Ashland)
Habitat for Humanity of Metro
Louisville
Northern Kentucky Habitat for Hu-
manity (Newport/Covington)
Paducah Habitat for Humanity
Woodford County Habitat for Hu-
manity (Midway)

Louisiana
Covington Habitat for Humanity
*Lafayette Parish Habitat for
Humanity (Lafayette)
New Orleans Area Habitat for Hu-
manity

Maine
Habitat for Humanity/Greater Port-
land
Habitat York County (Ogunquit)

Maryland
Chesapeake Habitat for Humanity
(Baltimore)
Garrett County Habitat for Human-
ity (Oakland)
Montgomery County Habitat for
Humanity (Rockville)

Massachusetts
Greater Lawrence Habitat for Humanity
Habitat Boston
Habitat for Humanity of Beverly
Habitat Worcester
South Shore Habitat for Humanity (Brockton/Norwell)

Michigan
Grand Rapids Habitat for Humanity
Habitat for Humanity of Metro Detroit
Kalamazoo Valley Habitat for Humanity
Lake County Habitat for Humanity (Baldwin)
Muskegon County Cooperating Churches Habitat for Humanity (Muskegon)

Minnesota
Twin Cities Habitat for Humanity (Minneapolis)

Mississippi
*Coahoma Habitat for Humanity
*Friars Point Habitat for Humanity
Holmes County Habitat for Humanity (Lexington)
*Jonestown Habitat for Humanity
Mississippi Delta Habitat for Humanity (Sumner)
Northeast Mississippi Habitat for Humanity (Tupelo)

Missouri
Habitat for Humanity/Missouri (Hayti)
Kansas City Habitat for Humanity

Nebraska
Omaha Habitat for Humanity

New Hampshire
Lakes Region Habitat for Humanity (Laconia)
Merrimack Habitat for Humanity (Warner)
New Hampshire Habitat for Humanity—Statewide umbrella organization (Manchester)

New Jersey
Gloucester County Habitat for Humanity (Pitman)
Jersey City Habitat for Humanity
Morris County Habitat for Humanity (Morristown)
Habitat for Humanity/Newark
Paterson Habitat for Humanity
Salem County Habitat for Humanity (Elmer)

New York
Cazenovia Area Habitat for Humanity
Flower City Habitat for Humanity (Rochester)
Habitat for Humanity/Buffalo
Habitat for Humanity of Suffolk County (Long Island)
Habitat for Humanity on the Lower East Side (New York)
Mid-Hudson Valley Habitat for Humanity (Poughkeepsie)
North Country Habitat for Humanity (Malone)
Syracuse Habitat for Humanity

North Carolina
Durham County Habitat for Humanity (Durham)
Habitat for Humanity of Catawba Valley (Hickory)
Habitat for Humanity of Charlotte
Habitat for Humanity of Forsyth County (Winston-Salem)
Heart of Carolina Habitat for Humanity (Raleigh)
Orange County Habitat (Chapel Hill)
Statesville-Iredell Habitat for Humanity (Statesville)
Thermal Belt Habitat for Humanity (Tryon)
Transylvania Habitat for Humanity (Brevard)
Western North Carolina Habitat for Humanity (Asheville)

Ohio
Ashland-Ironton Area Habitat (Ironton)
Dayton Habitat for Humanity
Wayne County Habitat for Humanity (Wooster)
Habitat for Humanity within Trumbull County (Warren)
Zanesville Habitat for Humanity

Oklahoma
Enid Habitat for Humanity

Oregon
Portland Habitat for Humanity

Pennsylvania
Greene County Habitat for Humanity (Waynesburg)
Habitat for Humanity/Greater Philadelphia
Habitat for Humanity in Harrisburg
Tri-County Pennsylvania Habitat for Humanity (State College)
York Habitat for Humanity

South Carolina
Central South Carolina Habitat for Humanity (Columbia)
Greenville County Habitat for Humanity (Greenville)
Oconee County Habitat for Humanity (Richland)
Pickens County Habitat for Humanity (Clemson)
Sea Island Habitat for Humanity (Johns Island)

Tennessee
Appalachia Habitat for Humanity (Robbins)
Habitat for Humanity of Jackson Area
Habitat for Humanity, Mid-South (Memphis)
Habitat for Humanity of Greater Chattanooga

Holston Habitat for Humanity (Kingsport)
Knoxville Habitat for Humanity
Nashville Area Habitat for Humanity

Texas
Amarillo Habitat for Humanity
Austin Habitat for Humanity
Beaumont Habitat for Humanity
Dallas Habitat for Humanity
Longview Habitat for Humanity
San Antonio Habitat for Humanity

Utah
Habitat for Humanity of Northern Utah (Brigham City)
Salt Lake Valley Habitat for Humanity (Salt Lake City)

Vermont
Green Mountain Habitat for Humanity (Burlington)
Upper Valley Habitat for Humanity (Quichee/White River Junction)

Virginia
Peninsula Habitat for Humanity (Newport News/Hampton)
New River Valley Habitat for Humanity (Christiansburg)

Washington
Buena Partners Habitat for Humanity (Zillah)
Seattle Habitat for Humanity
Tacoma-Pierce County Habitat for Humanity (Tacoma)

Wisconsin
Milwaukee Habitat for Humanity
Southwest Wisconsin Habitat for Humanity (Dodgeville)

Special Affiliate
Habitat for Handicapped Humanity (Milledgeville, GA)

*Provisional

Appendix E

Habitat for Humanity, International, Staff Roster

Executive
Millard Fuller, Director
Thomas E. Hall, Jr., Associate
Director
Linda Fuller, Assistant

Administrative
Karen Higgs, Director
Brenda Calloway, Office
Manager

Financial Services
Robert R. Geyer, Director

International Operations
Robert W. Stevens, Director
Clive Rainey, Africa
Coordinator
Kenneth L. Sauder, Latin
America and Haiti
Coordinator
Keith E. Branson, Asia and
Pacific Islands Coordinator

National Operations
Ted Swisher, Director
Barbara Baker, Assistant
Dale A. Hotelling, Assistant
Claire Williams, Assistant

Volunteer Services
Diane Nunnelee, Director
Carolyn Ross, Assistant

Development
D. Thomas Ford, Jr., Director
Bill Burnett, Assistant
Carol Pezzelli, Assistant

Media
Wallace Braud, Director
Nancy Braud, Editor, *Habitat
World*
Doralee F. Richardson, Print
Production Manager

Overseas Orientation
Susan Rhema, Director

Computer
Robert Geiger, Computers
Systems Manager
Paul Phillips, Information
Manager

Family Services
Grace Whitlock, Director
René Foster, Assistant

Construction
Kenneth L. Keefer, Foreman

Appendix F

Habitat for Humanity Directors and Advisors

An ecumenical Board of Directors and Board of Advisors guide the work of Habitat for Humanity. These dedicated folks raise funds, promote the work, travel all over the country at their own expense to attend meetings, and contribute their diverse skills in countless other ways.

Board of Directors

*Dr. David J. Rowe (President)
Melrose, MA
  American Baptist
Gordon Archibald, Hampton, NH
  Congregational
Dr. Robert Bratcher, Chapel Hill, NC
  Southern Baptist
Julia Marie Brown, Indianapolis, IN
  Disciples of Christ
Dr. Anthony Campolo, St. Davids, PA
  American Baptist
Jimmy Carter, Plains, GA
  Southern Baptist
*Pat Clark, Montgomery, AL
  American Baptist
*Bill Clarke, Canton, OH
  Presbyterian
Mary Emeny, Bushland, TX
  Ecumenical
*Lou Fischer, Jupiter, FL
  Roman Catholic
David Geiger, Rye, NY
  Presbyterian
*Dr. Robert Gemmer
St. Petersburg, FL
  Church of the Brethren
*Dr. Grover Hartman, Indianapolis, IN
  United Methodist

* Executive Committee Member

Mompongo Mo Imana, Ntondo, Zaire
  Baptist
Keith Jaspers, Springfield, MO
  United Methodist
Norma Kehrberg, New York, NY
  United Methodist
Robert Miller, East Cleveland, OH
  Presbyterian
*John Pritchard, Liberty, MO
  Presbyterian
Zenon Colque Rojas, Puno, Peru
  Roman Catholic
Larry Stoner, Lititz, PA
  Mennonite
Dr. Clyde Tilley, Jackson, TN
  Southern Baptist
Geoff Van Loucks, Los Gatos, CA
  United Church of Christ
Rosa Page Welch, Port Gibson, MS
  Disciples of Christ
Earl Wilson, Indianapolis, IN
  United Church of Christ
Andrew Young, Atlanta, GA
  United Church of Christ

Ex-Officio Member
George F. Anderson
Newmarket, Ontario, Canada
  United Church of Canada

Teddy Finney, Denver, CO
  Roman Catholic
Ron J. Foust, Americus, GA
  Roman Catholic
Roger Fredrickson, Wichita, KS
  American Baptist
Mark Frey, Kinshasa, Zaire
  United Church of Christ
Edgar Fuentes
Guatemala City, Guatemala
  Presbyterian
Myrna Gemmer, St. Petersburg, FL
  Church of the Brethren
P. V. George, Syracuse, NY
  United Church of Christ
Andrew Gibson, Midland, MI
  United Church of Christ
Jack Gilbert, Atlanta, GA
  United Methodist
Everett Gill, Stone Mountain, GA
  Southern Baptist
Rachel Gill, Stone Mountain, GA
  Southern Baptist
Joe Giron, Denver, CO
  Roman Catholic ·
Martha Beattie Graham, Brooklyn, NY
  Roman Catholic
Sandra Graham, Easley, SC
  Southern Baptist
Gertrude Greene, Savannah, GA
  Episcopal
Jim Griffin, Lexington, SC
  United Methodist
Jay Guffey, Springfield, MO
  United Methodist
Lisa Guffey, Springfield, MO
  United Methodist
Bruce C. Gunther, Atlanta, GA
  Episcopal
John Hager, Cape Coral, FL
  United Methodist
Ginny Handley, Gulu, Uganda
  United Church of Christ
Jim Handley, Gulu, Uganda ·
  United Church of Christ
Keith Harris, Richmond, VA
  Southern Baptist

Daryl Hartzler, Lake Odessa, MI
  United Methodist
Kay Hartzler, Lake Odessa, MI
  United Methodist
Clarie Collins Harvey, Jackson, MS
  United Methodist
Beth Heisey Kuttab, Jerusalem, Israel
  Brethren in Christ
Kenneth M. Henson, Jr., Columbus, GA
  United Methodist
Norman F. Heyl, Crofton, MD
  Presbyterian
Alice Howard, Salisbury, MD
  Presbyterian
Walden Howard, Salisbury, MD
  Presbyterian
Bobbie Hoy, Evansville, IN
  United Church of Christ
Raymond W. F. Hunt, Florence, AL
  Presbyterian
Pressley Ingram, Birmingham, AL
  United Church of Christ
Romando James, Clemson, SC
  Baptist
Lynwood B. Jenkins, Holland, PA
  Presbyterian
Patricia Johnson, Baconton, GA
  Baptist
Helen Kennedy, Lamar, IN
  United Church of Christ
Joe Hershberger Kirk, Millersburg, OH
  Mennonite
Loree Kirk, Waterford, MI
  United Church of Christ
Jonathan Knight, Syracuse, NY
  Presbyterian
Ronn B. Kreps, Minneapolis, MN
  Christian Reformed
Bruce Larson, Seattle, WA
  Presbyterian
Paul LaRue, Dallas, OR
  United Methodist
Janice DeRocker Ligon
Gloversville, NY
  Nondenominational
Ralph Loew, Buffalo, NY
  Lutheran

Bruno T. Lohrmann
Hendersonville, NC
Lutheran
Randall Lolley, Wake Forest, NC
Southern Baptist
Lou Lolley, Wake Forest, NC
Southern Baptist
Pedro Castro Lopez
Aguacatan, Guatemala
Evangelical
Sam Lott, Americus, GA
United Methodist
Faith Lytle, San Antonio, TX
Presbyterian
Ken MacHarg, Louisville, KY
United Church of Christ
Avery C. Manchester, New York, NY
United Methodist
Beth Marcus, New York, NY
Reformed Church
Carolyn Anne Martin, East Point, GA
Presbyterian
J. David Matthews, Winston-Salem, NC
Southern Baptist
Mary McCahon, Bayside, NY
Congregational
Don McClanen, Germantown, MD
Ecumenical
Julia McCray, Oakland, CA
Episcopal
Delores McMillin, Evansville, IN
Presbyterian
Joyce Millen, Akron, PA
Mennonite
John C. Miller, Paducah, KY
United Methodist
Roger Miller, Grand Junction, CO
United Church of Christ
Ed Moncrief, Salinas, CA
Roman Catholic
Don Mosley, Comer, GA
Ecumenical
Nick Negrete, Denver, CO
Reformed Church
Ann Nettum, Americus, GA
Episcopal
John Newell, Dayton, OH
American Baptist

Amy Olsen, State College, PA
Church of the Brethren
Bob Olsen, State College, PA
Church of the Brethren
Sandy Owen, Austin, TX
Disciples of Christ
George Percival, Santa Rosa, CA
United Church of Christ
Jim Perigo, Evansville, IN
United Church of Christ
John M. Perkins, Pasadena, CA
Interdenominational
Nancy Petrey, Southaven, MS
United Methodist
Barbara Philippart, Puno, Peru
Roman Catholic
Hubert C. Ping, Thorntown, IN
United Church of Christ
Michael Potter, Chapel Hill, NC
Ecumenical
Mary Pritchard, Liberty, MO
Presbyterian
Robert L. Rader, Ironton, OH
American Baptist
Debbie Ramey, Springfield, MO
United Methodist
Randy Ramey, Springfield, MO
United Methodist
Jim Ranck, Johns Island, SC
Mennonite
Diane Reed, Long Beach, CA
United Church of Christ
Neill Richards, New York, NY
United Church of Christ
Dan Roman, Mesa, AZ
American Baptist
Sally Roman, Mesa, AZ
American Baptist
Al Russell, Houston, TX
Disciples of Christ
Robert D. Samuelson, Memphis, TN
United Church of Christ
Audrey Sanders, Portland, OR
Disciples of Christ
William Charles Sanford, Atwater, CA
United Methodist
Harry Sangree, New York, NY
United Church of Christ

Sterling W. Schallert, Madison, WI
American Baptist

James F. Scherfee, Santa Rosa, CA
United Church of Christ

Charles Schultz, Wichita, KS
American Baptist

Mary Elizabeth Schumacher
Boulder, CO
Episcopal

Mason Schumacher, Boulder, CO
Episcopal

Wally Scofield, Westport, CT
Presbyterian

Diane Scott, Salem, NJ
American Baptist

Charles Selby, Old Fort, OH
United Methodist

John Sellars, Springfield, MO
Presbyterian

Marsha Sellars, Springfield, MO
Presbyterian

W. W. Sloan, Burlington, NC
United Church of Christ

Deen Day Smith, Norcross, GA
Southern Baptist

John Stahl-Wert, Elkhart, IN
Mennonite

Henry King Stanford, Americus, GA
United Methodist

Ted Stanley, Westport, CT
Ecumenical

Vada Stanley, Westport, CT
Ecumenical

John Staton, Green Bay, WI
United Church of Christ

George Steffey, Pittsburg, PA
United Church of Christ

Bernard Strasser, Ormond Beach, FL
Presbyterian

Christine Street, Marietta, GA
Episcopal

Kay Swicord, Brookeville, MD
Presbyterian

Jack Swisher, Cincinnati, OH
Presbyterian

Jack Takayanagi, Portland, OR
United Church of Christ

Donald Tarr, Salinas, CA
United Methodist

George N. Theuer, Americus, GA
United Methodist

Chuck Thomas, Cartersville, GA
Episcopal

Linda Thomas, Cartersville, GA
Episcopal

Barbara Thompson, Brevard, NC
Baptist

Rhodes Thompson, Enid, OK
Disciples of Christ

Leonard L. Tillett, Norwich, England
Congregational

Nancy Tilley, Jackson, TN
Southern Baptist

Franklin Townsend, Lake Odessa, MI
Church of the Brethren

Charles (Bo) Turner, Clarkesville, GA
Southern Baptist

Lorne J. Twiner, Cummings, GA
Roman Catholic

Delores Van Loucks, Los Gatos, CA
United Church of Christ

Jack VandenHengel, Baltimore, MD
Southern Baptist

Anton J. Vroon, Kalamazoo, MI
Reformed Church

Carl Walker, Kalamazoo, MI
United Methodist

Charles Warren, Atlanta, GA
Southern Baptist

Cynthia Wedel, Alexandria, VA
Episcopal

Mel West, Columbia, MO
United Methodist

W. James White, Morristown, NJ
United Methodist

Ralph Whittenburg, South Bend, IN
Lutheran

Bill Wiley, Jewett, OH
Presbyterian

Jack Wolters, Columbus, NC
United Church of Christ

Lois Wolters, Columbus, NC
United Church of Christ

Donald Yates, Terre Haute, IN
Community Church

Madonna Yates, Terre Haute, IN
  Community Church
Ronald Yates, Acton, MA
  United Church of Christ
John Yeatman, El Cajon, CA
  American Baptist

Jean C. Young, Atlanta, GA
  United Church of Christ
Dave Yutzy, Plain City, OH
  Mennonite
Ben Zaglaniczny, Fort Myers, FL
  Roman Catholic

Appendix G

Habitat for Humanity Volunteers

Overseas Volunteers (1973–1986)

Africa:

Nzoia Community, Kenya
Marjorie Fox
Paul Haddad
Dan Haling
Karen & Mark Lassman-Eul
Hugh O'Brien
Susan & Dan Rhema, Sydel

Lilongwe, Malawi
Dan Haling
Elma & Miles Richmond, Paula
and Micah

Gulu, Uganda
Hulen & Wil Brown
Paul Haddad
Ginny & Jim Handley
Clive Rainey
Patrick Welch
Joseph Wheeler
Paula Young

Basankusu, Zaire
Gil Blaisdell
Bill Clifton
Erasmus Meinerts

Bikoro, Zaire
Marian Rose

Gemena, Zaire
Barbara & Greg Garrett
Alice Miller
Pixi & Phill Phillips, Kem, Christi,
and Lorenza

Ikoko Bonginda, Zaire
R. Dean DeBoer
Larry Hart
Beth & Ken Reno, Melissa

Kikwit, Zaire
Jan & David Byerlee, Sara Jo
Phyllis & Glen Boese, Steve
Norma Ueleke

Kinshasa, Zaire
Ken Braun
Jan & David Byerlee, Sara Jo
and Paxton
Chuck Clark
Leon Emmert
Margee & Mark Frey, Matthew
and Meredith
Larry Hart
Robbie MacDonald
Clive Rainey
Beth & Ken Reno, Melissa and
Jonathan
Christian Sheline
Joy & Cliff Stabell
Anne Westman
John Yeatman

Lake Tumba Area, Zaire
R. Dean DeBoer
Laura Freeland
Rex Gardner
Larry Hart
Marian Rose
Phil Steinkamp
Joe Talento

Mbandaka, Zaire
Jan & Howard Caskey
Chuck Clark
Pat Clark
Karen Foreman
Dan Froese

Linda & Millard Fuller, Chris,
   Kim, Faith, and Georgia
Luanne & Harry Goodall
Ken Harris
Pressley Ingram
Joe Kirk
Martine Lihoreau
Dale Long
Bruce McCrae
Cindy Miller
Roger Miller
Jeff Moger
Don Mosley
Ron Prior
Dan Roman
Harry Sangree
Ken Sauder
Mary Schroeder
David Seely
Christian Sheline
Larry Stoner
Bonnie Watson

Ntondo, Zaire
Jeff Buttram
Pat Clark
Peter Clarke
Bill Clifton
Beth Corbitt
Jane & Ralph Gnann, Sidney
   and John
Karen & Ryan Karis
Mitch Kjose
Peter Kratzat
Ronn Kreps
Janet Lekrone
Dodie & Chris Lepp, Topher
Dale Long
Donna & David Moss, Rachel
   and Laura
Debbie Pfau
Beth & Ken Reno, Melissa
Dan Roman
Dana Rominger
Mark Rylance
Ken Sauder
Perry Schempp
Connie & Bill Ward

Chanyanya, Zambia
Bill Allison
Kay & Bob Olson
Kabuyu Island, Zambia
Bill Allison
Lee Chaudoin

Asia:

Khammam, India
Barbara & Roger Sneller, Abbey
   and Anjuli
Papua New Guinea
Ann & John Franken
Evelyn & Gordon Lange
John Spratt

Caribbean:

Dumay, Haiti
Rob DeRocker
Eleanor Frank
Stephanie & Lance Fryholm-
   Cheslock
Pam & Carl Hanson, Ian
John Liacos
Robert Lieske
Tim Rockwell
Art Russell

Latin America:

Alto Beni, Bolivia
Larry Godeke
Steven Robertshaw
Luke Stollings

Aguacatan, Guatemala
Diane & Lowell Birkey
Keith Branson
Kitty Brown
Dick Perry
Steve Salva
Becky & David Sheill
Betty Jo & Bob Stevens, Michelle
   and Eric
German Pomares, Nicaragua
Susan Bailey
Sarah & Jim Hornsby, Matthew
Tom Klein

Julie Knop
Cory Scholtes

Matagalpa, Nicaragua
Carole Harper & Mike Prentiss

Juliaca, Peru
Debbie & Andy Kramer, Eric,
Wesley, and Jessee
Peter Shaw
Bret Stein

Manazo, Peru
Ann Bancroft

Puno, Peru
Keith Branson
Elvin Compy, Nick
Ginny & Miller Lovett
Susan & Dan Rhema, Sydel
Peter Shaw
Nancy Straus
Chichi & Ken VanDyke, Ross
and Danielle

Long-Term Volunteers in the International Office
(who served one year or more)

Bob & Joanne Avers
Barbara Baker
Gary & Linda Bergh,
Susan and David
Roy & Evelyn Bickley
Kevin Bowers
Wallace & Nancy Braud
JoAnn Brenneman
Trish Bryan
Beth Buley
Bill & Joan Burnett
Perry Bush
Albert Campanella
Judi Carpenter
Lee Chaudoin
Jim Chaney
David Conley
Joe & Rose Crowley
Martha Cruz
Paul & Kathie DuPont,
Jennifer, Lisa, and
Kevin
John Eden
Dave Enting
Joy Esbenshade
Rene Foster
Linda Fuller
Barbara Garvin
Bob & Kathy Geyer,
Scott and Matthew
Gerry Glynn
Patti & Gene Grier

Wilbur & Elizabeth
Hershberger, Anna,
Maria, Sarah, and
Rachel
Marlene Hess
Clarence Hollis
Bob & Joyce Hooley-
Gingrich
Phil Hoy
David Hovestol
David Hungerford
Sue Ice
David Jones
David & Mary Joseph
Ken & Nancy Keefer,
Megan and Joshua
Jane Kennedy
Loree Kirk
David Kreider
Aafke Kruizinga
David Langdon
Willie Laster
Cleta Lee
Ruth Lindsey
Kika Loucaides
Robbie MacDonald
Amy Martel
Solomon & Sarah
Maendel, Keith,
Steve, Karen, Mark,
Eleanor, and Timothy
Julia McCray

Carolyn McGarity
Noel & Gloria Miller
Dennis & Vert Miller
Bill & Amy Moore
Don & Faye Nice
Kaye Noffsinger
Cindy Nolt
Hugh O'Brien
Sue Oths
Joel Palmquist
Amy Parsons
Ron Prior
Guy Patrick
Janette Prickett
Clive Rainey
Laurie Riggs
Dan Riley
Carolyn Ross
Fran Seaver
Fred Schippert
Cory Scholtes
Joyce Schwartz
David & Becky Sheill,
Matthew
Steve Sheridan & Anne
Tabor
Dan & Rachel Shinkle
Bev Showalter
Amber Smith
John Spratt
Bill Smith
Nancy Straus

Donna Stevens	Carl Vogel	Jack Westfall
Ellen Studley	Anita Wallace	Grace Whitlock
Judy Szbara	Brian Warford	Leon Wilburn
Pete Talboys	Brian Weaver	Claire Williams
Carl Thomas	Tom & Lynn Webster,	Tim & Elizabeth Wilson
Tom Trainor	Corey and K. C.	Mark Wright
Ed Vennell	Sue West	Steve Zale

For further information about Habitat for Humanity, write or call:

Habitat for Humanity
Habitat & Church Streets
Americus, GA 31709–3423
(912) 924–6935

Other books about the ministry of Habitat for Humanity are available at the above address:

Community Self-Help Housing Manual   Helpful, detailed information regarding the steps (philosophical and practical) involved in starting an affiliated Habitat project.

Kingdom Building: Essays from the Grassroots of Habitat   A collection of writings about the vision of Habitat and its implementation, as seen through the eyes of partners and volunteers in the U.S. and other countries.

Bokotola   Habitat's beginnings as a housing ministry in Mbandaka, Zaire, and the vision of providing decent housing for God's people in need all over the world. Told by Millard Fuller.

Love in the Mortar Joints   The story of Habitat for Humanity's first four years of growth; the launching of sixteen projects in North America, Africa and Central America. Recounted by Millard Fuller and Diane Scott.

Photo by Vern Ogrodnek

MILLARD FULLER, lawyer and former businessman, is founder and executive director of the nonprofit organization Habitat for Humanity. The Fullers have served as missionaries to Africa as well as to the slums of America, and are spreading "Jesus economics" all over the world. Millard, author of *Bokotola* and *Love in the Mortar Joints,* spends much of his time speaking to audiences all across the country raising support for Habitat. Millard and Linda Fuller have four children: Chris, Kim, Faith, and Georgia. The Fullers live in Americus, Georgia.

DIANE SCOTT is a free lance writer in Salem, New Jersey, where she and her husband, Victor, own and operate a nursery farm. The Scotts are longtime supporters of Habitat and serve on the board of Salem County Habitat for Humanity. Diane is also on Habitat's international advisory board. She has published numerous magazine articles, and she assisted Millard with his two previous books. The Scotts have three children: Ellen, Wendy, and Kevin.